The Disappearance
Of Goldie Rapaport

By Evelyn Julia Kent

Based On The Memories
Of Gina Schwarzmann

For Neil and Family,
With my best wishes for 5778.
Shana Tova!
Evelyn Julia Kent.

Published in 1994
Second Edition 2017 by:
Evelyn Julia Kent

ISBN: 978-0-9523716-5-6

Printed and bound in Great Britain by:
Book Printing UK, Remus House, Coltsfoot Drive, Woodston,
Peterborough PE2 9BF

*Author's note: This is a true story. As it is told from memory, some
of the names and incidental details may not be quite accurate.*

In loving memory of my mother, Rachel Rapaport,
who perished in the Shoah aged 31.
A symbol of courage.
Her kindness, dignity and charm
will always be cherished.

Gina Schwarzmann

IN MEMORY OF GRANDFATHER

In the shadow of the pogroms, he was proud of being a Jew. His whole life was a symbolic act. Every gesture, every prayer, was so charged with meaning that his heart overflowed with the beauty and the tragedy of creation.

At first the Jews were welcome in Eastern Europe: a relatively backward region, which was happy to have immigrants experienced in commerce and the industrial arts. Poland, especially, offered them religious freedom and the right to run their own communities.

So thankfully they settled down – with their religion, their language, their customs and their exalted sense that all life is holy. During the subsequent eight hundred years, they built an unworldly, unregarded way of life which we shall miss.

For centuries, Jews had learned to follow the precepts of Micah, where they had learned that the greatest sin on earth is callousness to suffering and that charity is not an option but a command and where they had built a life round the advice of Joshua to study the Torah 'day and night'.

Clearly, there was no room for people like this in the thousand-year Reich which the Germans were planning.

(Herbert Agar – The Saving Remnant:
An account of Jewish Survival since 1914 – Rupert Hart-Davis
1960)

CONTENTS

Acknowledgements

Preface

ACKNOWLEDGEMENTS

We wish to thank our colleagues, friends and family who have helped us keep faith with this project. We are indebted to David Morgan and Sidney Larholt for their computer expertise; to Michael Davies for his scholarly time-scale of events; to Hazel Davies and Pat Healy for proofreading; to John O'Toole for his sympathetic editing; to Andrew Nurnberg for his interest and advice, and Jennifer Lipman for her illustrations.

Particular thanks are due to David Schwarzmann and Frank Entwistle who have supported us throughout with patience, sound advice and practical help.

Also thanks are due to Moe Kanareck, editor and life long friend.

Finally our love and thanks to go Mira Kalwasinski and Professor Stefan Grudzinski for their notes and recollections, and to the whole Grudzinski family whose courage and fortitude epitomizes the stand of good against evil.

PREFACE

When democracy came to Poland, early in 1990, Gina felt there was now nothing to stop her returning to Warsaw and retracing her journey to Radom. Her daughter, Rachelle, and friend, Evelyn, agreed to accompany her.

It was an emotional trip. The British Airways aeroplane was packed with Jewish Youth on their way to join a worldwide 'March of the Living' to Auschwitz, in the commemoration of the six million Jews slaughtered in the Holocaust.

At Warsaw Airport, Mira and Sebastian Kalwasinski were waiting with smiles and tears to welcome their 'Genia' home. They embraced in joyful reunion. Gina spoke in pure Polish as if she had never been away.

The following morning, Sebastian packed everyone into his car to follow the flat, ancient road to Radom. Gina was full of intense excitement. Almost before the car was parked in the square she set off, full of determination, through the park to the other side of Radom with the rest following her quickening footsteps.

The wooden footbridge she had expected to see spanning the railway line was no longer there. Instead, there was a motorway carrying roaring traffic. Undeterred, she found a pedestrian underpass which led out into a street she recognised.

Curious locals came forward to help these strangers with directions, but Gina knew where she was. She had found her Grandfather's timber yard. Part had been built over and part was now a car repair lot, but one mechanic remembered the original yard and the three log cabins long ago pulled down.

Gina looked around, remembering her past. Rachelle took photographs of the house that had once been home to her family. Evelyn stood deep in thought that a tale worth telling had begun here fifty years ago.

PART ONE

RADOM TO WARSAW

1. THE FOREST

Autumn 1938

Autumn in Poland often brought gales and frost but on the special day that I remember the air was clean and bright. Birch trees and elms were shedding their leaves to be ready for the harsh winter. Russet and golden shapes floated down softly carpeting the forest paths. The pines stood tall and calm. Shadows played in the pale sunlight. It was a living forest full of hidden creatures that dwelt in the region of Garbatka.

I danced along beside my Grandfather, enjoying the rustle of the leaves under my galoshes. I wore a snug, woollen, brown coat and my long, golden plaits, tied with red ribbon, bounced around my shoulders.

Suddenly Grandfather stopped and put a finger to his bearded lips. He pointed to the quivering tail of a squirrel as it froze against a tree trunk.

'Look, Goldie, see the colour of the squirrel? See how it blends in with the trunk. The tree is its shelter and home, its food store and friend. A living tree . . .' he said reverently. 'Like the Torah, a Tree of Life.'

We stood quite still for a moment holding our breath, hearing the alarm call of birds warning of our approach and catching the sound of small animals scuffling away into the undergrowth. My eyes sparkled with the curiosity of a four-year-old.

Grandfather picked a large, ripe fruit from the bramble and carefully inspected it.

'Here is a delicious meal!' he said, popping it into my mouth. It tasted sweet and succulent.

Then he led me over to a silver birch.

'See the sheen on this bark? Just feel it,' he said, running his hand lovingly along the trunk.

He placed my hand on the tree for my small fingers to explore the texture.

2

'And here,' he went on excitedly, moving over to a nearby elm. 'Look at the moss around the base, so smooth and rich, just like a lady's green velvet collar.'

He pointed to deep green ivy that grew high around some trees like soft, swathed robes.

'They're dressed in their Sunday best,' he chuckled, his kindly, grey eyes shining with tenderness for me as we shared the delights of the forest.

He loved nature and knew about many different kinds of trees. After all, that was his business. He was the owner of a large timber yard on the outskirts of Radom, buying and selling the stacks of pine, oak and elm that lay weathering in his grounds beside the three log cabins.

Later, we sat together on the base of a felled tree and he showed me how to count the rings.

'This is an old tree,' he said. 'Over one hundred years.'

'Why did they cut it down?'

I always wanted answers to everything.

'Because its time had come to be useful in another way,' he replied, thoughtfully. 'Nothing is forever, Goldie.'

Before returning to Radom, Grandfather settled his dealing with the foresters and I had to wait impatiently, scuffing the ground like the horses, longing to have him to myself again.

At long last, I was scooped up to the front seat of the cart by Zygmund, Grandfather's foreman, to sit snugly between them as the horses plodded solidly along. They were strong, docile creatures. A chestnut mare called Kasztan, nodding her head in the reins next to silver-white Srebro, who swished his straw-coloured tail at me. The drive took us back through the flat, Polish countryside.

From my vantage point, I could see peasants working in the open fields for cabbages and cereals.

As the cart trundled through small villages, folk greeted us. Zygmund would yell back any news, but to Grandfather they always said, 'Dzien dobry, pan.' (Good morning, sir.)

3

Grandfather nodded and waved a greeting. Even though his own language was Yiddish (and he prayed in Hebrew) he spoke fluent Polish. He was looked upon as a holy man. Many Jews and non-Jews came to him for advice and help. They called him affectionately Rov (Rabbi) because he was wise. Truly wise. People would come upon him in his home, sitting at his huge desk contemplating holy books, calmly stroking his silky, grey beard with his fine, strong hands, often deep in prayer.

At the end of the journey, Zygmund lovingly tended the horses whilst I followed Grandfather into the warmth of his log cabin. He lived in the largest chalet with the youngest of his six children, Sarah, who was my Aunt (Chucha).

Zygmund lived nearby in a smaller log cabin with his wife and little daughter, Basia. He was Grandfather's main helpmate, running the business, supplying wood to the nearby munitions factory. He was strong enough to stack great piles of timber outside in the yard to weather. Rare woods, such as mahogany and walnut were housed in the third log cabin.

Once inside Grandfather's home, I ran to the windows, eager to open the delicate, pinewood shutters that Zygmund had carved during the long, dark, winter evenings.

Later, after we had finished the delicious potato soup that Chucha had left on the stove for us, I sat, trailing my fingers around the trellised pattern on the shutters. I did not interrupt Zygmund and Grandfather as they discussed the day's business, sitting together at the huge, wooden desk strewn with books and papers. They chatted and laughed. They seemed to have great respect for each other, even though they came from such different backgrounds and religions. After all, Zygmund was a devout Roman Catholic like most of the Polish people, whereas Grandfather was Jewish.

They were both very patient with me and my questions. Why this? Why that? They seemed to be able to order my world. I loved them both, but no one anywhere made me feel as safe as Grandfather.

4

My visits to the timber yard always ended too soon for me. When my mother (Mamushia) called on the way home from working in the family bakery to collect me, I sighed.

'I wish I could live with Grandfather forever!'

'That's only because he spoils you,' said Mamushia fondly.

'He gives me potatoes with cream and chives, it's so delicious I could just live on it forever! Besides, he teaches me things, all about the forest.'

'Well, there are other things besides the forest you need to learn about,' said Mamushia tartly. 'You will soon be going to school.'

I pulled a face. I was not sure that I wanted to learn from anybody else except Grandfather.

2. RADOM

On the way home to our apartment at Zeromskiego 21, we called at Mr Lipinski's grocery shop to buy provisions. Delicious smells of pickled herrings and cheeses pervaded the store and made my nose itch with pleasure. I liked Mr Lipinski because he always managed to secretly give me something to taste, but this evening I was disappointed as it was his housekeeper, Janina, serving behind the counter and she and Mamushia always chatted for ages.

'We need cream cheese and pickled cucumbers for this evening,' Mamushia said, 'and have you heard the latest . . .?'

I wandered outside, not resisting the temptation to push my little fingers into the open sacks of grain by the front door. Mr Lipinski's hand suddenly came from nowhere, caught me by the collar and turned me around. I gasped, but he bent down and winked at me before guiding me back into his store and finding me a barley sugar.

After that, Mamushia and I made our way through the park to the other side of Radom. It was almost dusk, but children were out playing on the swings, screaming and yelling to each other. We came out near a smart street dotted with small, exclusive shops. I could see into the café, already brightly lit, where customers sat chatting, men smoking their pipes and playing cards or chess.

We passed the bathhouse where, twice a week, I went with Mamushia and Chucha. Here we could rent a white-tiled bathroom with steaming hot water, soap and warm towels. We would take it in turns to have a bath. Firstly, I was washed and dried then, while Mamushia had her bath, I sat in the warm waiting room with Chucha, who briskly rubbed my long, fair hair dry before combing and plaiting it with red ribbon before she had her turn.

Afterwards, wrapped up well so as not to catch cold, we would walk over to the café for cakes and Bavarka. Ladies sipped piping-hot, lemon tea through a lump of sugar in their

6

mouths (just like the Russians) whilst I swung my legs under the chair and drank sweet, warm milk.

I held tightly on to Mamushia's warm hand as we turned into a darkening passageway leading to Zeromskiego 21, where we climbed the wooden stairs to our apartment.

Inside, yellow and white curtains draped the windows, making it appear light and sunny, even in winter. Mamushia loved flowers and filled vases in all the rooms with blooms or greenery.

She bent down to help me take off my galoshes and I could see her beautiful, long, black hair neatly combed into a bun at the nape of her neck. People said she looked more French than Polish, tall and slim and always elegant in her smart, bright clothes, enhanced by a cameo brooch or an amber necklace. She was lovely.

'Heads turn when Rachel walks,' said Grandfather proudly of his beautiful daughter, my mother.

'Run along and get ready for bed,' said Mamushia as she took off her coat.

My heart sank.

'But I want to wait up for Tatush!' I cried.

I rarely saw him these days.

My father, Simon Rapaport, was an energetic, good-looking, young man who had fallen in love with Mamushia and married her – even though she was his cousin and the family disapproved. I was their only child, but sometimes I felt I was a disappointment to him because I was not a boy.

'Please, Goldie, be a good girl and undress yourself,' pleaded Mamushia. 'Daddy won't be in yet. He's seeing Mr Bombala about business matters. He told me he would be very late.'

Nowadays, Tatush was always busy running his business, importing goods from Germany and having meetings with business associates. He did not seem to have any time for me at all.

'Come along, darling. Quickly to bed . . . I have people coming for a Zionist meeting tonight.'

'What's it for?'

I hung back as long as possible.

'We're people who want to go and live in Palestine.' She looked at me intently with her deep brown eyes. 'To Jerusalem.'

I opened and closed my mouth without saying that I did not want to go to Jerusalem or anywhere else away from Grandfather. I stumped off to my room.

'Well, I'll ask Basia to play tomorrow,' I called out, longing for company.

Apart from my cousins, my one, true friend was Basia, Zygmund's daughter. We played in the timber yard together, sharing secrets, collecting leaves, stones and bits of wood shavings for playing shopkeepers, pretending to be Mr Lipinski and Janina serving customers.

Alone in my bedroom, I sat disconsolately on the bed as visitors arrived. Then Chucha's head appeared around the door. With fingers to her lips, she tiptoed in like a conspirator and handed me a cookie and a piece of chocolate. It was just like a midnight feast! I felt a great surge of love for her and suddenly I thought how lucky I was to be part of the Rapaport family.

* * * * *

September 1939

At last came the day of starting school. I felt fearful and excited at the same time. Mamushia walked me the half-mile through the park to the timber yard to collect Basia, since it was her first morning at school as well.

There was not a cloud in the sky as we two friends walked hand in hand through the school gates to join other children eagerly crowding into the classroom, rushing to find seats.

'Sit next to me, Goldie,' pleaded Basia.

'We'll always be friends, won't we?'

I was feeling strangely grown-up, sitting at a desk.

'Of course we will. My papa loves Rov Rapaport, my mother loves your family and I love you. So we are bound to stay friends forever,' said Basia with complete confidence.

At noon each day, after morning lessons, we skipped home for dinner. The midday meal was the largest of the day. There were always three courses: soup, meat and vegetables, followed by pudding. If Mamushia happened to be working in the family bakery that day, I would eat with Grandfather. Otherwise, when she was home, she often allowed Basia to come back to the apartment with me. Basia was completely intrigued by our proper, flush toilet because the one in the timber yard was in a primitive hut and stank horribly.

Back at school in the afternoon, we had games, music or art. Whatever we did, Basia and I stayed near to each other. Even after school, we played in each other's homes until suppertime.

*   *   *   *   *

But, unknown to us, evil happenings were taking place in the world beyond Radom. The Germans had taken over Poland and were making strict rules about Jews. In Radom, on 16th December, posters were pinned to walls announcing that all Jews and their children over the age of ten must wear a white band with a blue star on their right arm. They were not allowed to use bathhouses any more. Property of the Jews was being confiscated. Without warning, my whole world was coming apart.

Mamushia sat white-faced by the radio, listening to the announcements.

Tatush came in early and I rushed up to him crying, 'Why? Why?'

I begged him to explain what was happening, but the more I asked, the more angry he became.

'Don't keep asking me why. I don't know why! Everybody has to do it,' he shouted.

Worst of all, next morning, when I arrived with Mamushia to collect Basia for school, she refused to go with us. I hurt with desolation. As I reached the gates, Basia was with a crowd of others jeering at me and I had to go in alone.

'Get away from me, you Jewess!' Basia screamed in the classroom.

I stood there stunned, trembling with shock at the look of hatred on her face.

'Please, Basia, I'm your best friend,' I pleaded, tears welling up.

'No, you're not!' she shouted. 'I'm with the others in school . . . and we don't want you Jews.'

Basia had removed herself from our desk, leaving me to sit alone. I had no idea what I had done to deserve this treatment. Why did the others despise me so? Why was being Jewish so terrible? I knew I did not look any different from other Polish children, I did not feel any different, so what was it that made me different?

'Goldie Rapaport!'

The teacher's voice interrupted my thoughts.

'Take your books and go sit at that desk at the back of the class . . . away from the others.'

Miss must have heard the radio too about how Jews were to be treated.

The headmaster came into the classroom just before dinner break.

'Stand up all you Jewish children,' he ordered, looking at me and the two boys sat at the back.

We stood up sheepishly.

'Now, class, see these Jews? They killed Jesus. That is why they are pigs and not human, so you know what we think of them!'

Loud jeering came from the class. The head stood with his arms folded, nodding approval.

I was indignant. Who was Jesus? I wondered. And how could I have killed him?

I cried out, 'I don't know Jesus and I've never killed anyone!'

Boys threw rubbers at us as we Jewish children stood, bewildered at such an accusation. One hit me and stung my cheek which made me start to cry just as the bell rang for midday break. I ran out to Mamushia and threw myself at her, sobbing uncontrollably.

She took me home the long way and comforted me, but she hardly understood what was happening either. I absolutely refused to go back that day.

'I will speak to the teacher tomorrow,' she promised.

'But who is Jesus? Why do they say I killed him?'

'You haven't done any such thing. It all happened nearly two thousand years ago. It wasn't the Jews who killed Jesus, it was the Romans. It has nothing to do with you, darling,' said Mamushia cuddling me and weeping too. 'It has to do with wicked people called Nazis.'

That night I cried myself to sleep. A terrible nightmare haunted me where I was trapped in a cage with leering faces peering in on me. I tried, but could not escape. I woke screaming as Tatush came into my bedroom and sat on my bed. It was one of the few occasions he seemed to have time for me. He listened patiently as I related the awful things that had happened.

'Goldie, there's great evil surrounding us. I can't stop it happening, but I'll do all in my power to keep it away from you.'

He squeezed my hand and stood up.

'I'll have a word with Zygmund about Basia,' he said. 'Now, go back to sleep.'

He stopped by the door and looked back at me, peeping from under the blankets.

'Thank God you are a girl,' he murmured, almost to himself. 'If you were a boy, nothing could save you.'

Next morning Mamushia took me right into the classroom and spoke to the teacher.

11

'She's a good little girl,' the teacher nodded at me, 'and very bright.'

She looked somewhat ashamed as she went on . . . 'But I can't help it if the other children don't like her.'

Basia flatly refused to sit next to me or have anything to do with me, but Zygmund must have spoken to her because she stopped yelling out names.

For the last week of the Christmas term, I stood alone in the playground, watching forlornly as my friend Basia played with other children.

* * * * *

23 January 1940

Mamushia gave me a special hug on this morning. It was my sixth birthday and I was given a new pair of shoes, shiny, brown, lace-ups, and some bright red, tartan material for a pretty dress. My cousins, Jacob and Isaac, Renia and Samuel, came round to see me and play in my bedroom while the grown-ups discussed the worsening situation.

The weather was bitterly cold but the climate for Jews under the Nazi regime was becoming even more unbearable. Tatush was unable to carry on his business although he managed to sort something out with Mr Bombala so that he could have money. The family bakery was still running, but food was getting so scarce that long queues formed, often starting at midnight to be sure of bread.

There was no thought of my going back to school. I spent more time than ever with Grandfather in his log cabin, sitting by the window, watching the snowflakes drift down. By the middle of February, the wind began to whip up the snow, sending swirls of white cloud around the timber yard. Stacks of wood were piled under deep sheets of snow.

Zygmund dug pathways whilst I helped Grandfather sprinkle wood shavings along them to make walking safer.

There were plenty of logs for the fire and the storehouse was full of potatoes, onions and carrots. Danger seemed far away. I enjoyed the special feeling of being snug and well fed whilst the wind howled outside, banging loose boards and buffeting the trees.

'Poor trees!' I sighed.

Grandfather chuckled. 'They stand like sentinels. They're well prepared for winter storms, don't you worry. They sleep now, waiting for the harshness to come, but when spring arrives they'll live again. Nature renews itself,' he said, pulling me closer to him. 'Everything lives again.'

He helped me into my warm coat and gathered his prayer shawl.

'Come, it will soon be Sabbath,' he observed. 'I'll walk you home on my way to prayers.'

Grandfather left me at the doorway to the apartment. I ran up the stairs making such a clatter that Mamushia opened the door before I reached the top.

'Take off your galoshes, hang your coat up neatly and wash your hands,' she said, smiling. 'And then you can put the chola on the table ready for Sabbath.'

Everything inside the flat was neat and tidy, ready for Sabbath. Chucha was already there and a delicious smell of frying drifted from the kitchen. I did as I was told before collecting the plaited loaf from the bread bin and placing it on a silver breadboard. I set it on the dining table, carefully covering the chola with a pretty, white lace cloth. The candles stood tall and unlit, waiting to make their welcoming glow.

Every Friday night, I was enchanted when Mamushia lit the candles and covered her eyes with her delicate hands to say a silent prayer. Then Grandfather would return from synagogue, cover his head with a small, white cap, smooth down his long, silky beard and sing a blessing over a cup of wine before it was passed around. I had a tiny sip at the end.

Just as I was about to fetch the kosher wine and silver goblet for Grandfather's blessing, there was a knock at the front door and I could hear the startled, stifled cries of Mamushia and Chucha.

I ran into the hallway and there stood Grandfather, but I scarcely recognised him. He was covered in mud. His face was cut below the eye, blood trickled down his cheek . . . and his beard, his long, silky beard was no longer there. It had been chopped off in clumps and all that was left were some patches of grey stubble sticking out from his bleeding chin.

'What's happened?' I screamed, throwing myself at him.

'Ah, let me collect myself. Help me to get out of this,' he said, gently pushing me aside.

He painfully removed his overcoat as Mamushia hurried to fetch some warm water to sponge away the blood.

He sank into an armchair.

'There were four of them,' he gasped. 'Ruffians, thugs. They took hold of me, threw me down, held me down and cut off my beard.'

His hand went to stroke where his beard had been.

'I suppose they were drunkards,' said Chucha, handing him a glass of brandy.

'No.' Grandfather shook his head sadly. 'If they were drunk, tomorrow they might regret knocking down an old man. No, no, these were Nazis. They were enjoying themselves.'

'What are we to do?' wailed Mamushia.

By the time Tatush appeared, Grandfather had cleaned up and shaved off the rest of his beard before the candles were lit. It was a sombre Friday night meal. Afterwards, when I had gone to bed, the adults discussed what was to be done. But there was little that could be done.

During the following weeks, everyone was scared because more laws against Jews came into force. They were forbidden to own property or businesses. They were not allowed to walk in parks or even on the pavements. They had to stay away from the centre of towns. Maps were posted on walls describing the only areas where Jews were allowed to live. There was nothing to be done except obey. German soldiers were moving into Radom in force.

By the beginning of March, my whole family joined the Jewish community of Radom, converging on the Ghetto, a square mile of land next to the railway line where we were permitted to live. Everyone's belongings had to be left behind except what they could put on one cart, or push in a pram, or carry in bundles.

Grandfather gave the timber yard to Zygmund. They decided to stack two log cabins with stocks of wood to prevent German soldiers billeting there. Zygmund, his wife and Basia, went into Grandfather's log house. My father's business associate, Mr Bombala and his family, moved into our apartment to look after it.

In the Ghetto, my uncles and their families found places to live. Grandfather and Chucha moved into a room nearby whilst Tatush rented a storeroom for us. It all happened so quickly. By the end of March 1940, my home was just in one room at the back of a corner drapery shop at number 6 Walowa Street, in the Radom Ghetto.

3. THE GHETTO

Six Walowa Street was the corner shop that stood just behind the white wall separating the Ghetto from the rest of Radom. The owner of the shop was Old Ma Becky, a stern, upright, elderly woman with grey hair in a huge bun at the back of her neck. She had two old maids for daughters and ruled them with a rod of iron, so it was no wonder they were sullen and unsmiling.

But she excelled as a shopkeeper. Her small store was the neatest, most fascinating shop I had ever been in. It was full of coloured ribbons and wools, reels of cotton and skeins of silk. Every kind of sewing material was stored in tiny, brown drawers that lined the walls and went along the counter. Each section was neatly labelled: pins, hatpins, needless, knitting needles, tape, measuring tape, elastic, buckram, tapestry canvas and buttons. To a bright and curious little girl the shop was full of treasure.

Every morning I skipped in looking for something new to touch. Even though I could just read, words like 'twill' or 'embroidery' confused me so the contents of the drawers often came as quite a surprise. It was a fascinating game to pull them open and find pearl buttons in sections of different sizes, or bright skeins of embroidery silks arranged in rainbow colours. I could hardly keep my hands off the rows of coloured cotton reels or the layers of bright tissue paper.

The minute Old Ma Becky spotted me touching something she yelled, 'Don't play with that! Into the corner with you!'

I scampered away, but she soon relented enough to lift me on to her lap for a cuddle.

'I've always wanted a little granddaughter just like you,' she said, sniffing loudly at the thought of her spinster daughters. 'But there's not much hope of that!'

She set me down and I watched her select coloured buttons which she dropped into a small box.

'There you are,' she said. 'Play with these, count them . . . if you can.'

16

'Oh, thank you!' I gasped. 'They will be my special treasure . . . please . . . may I have just one large, pearly button for very best?'

After that I sat quietly in the corner happily making patterns with them on the floor.

Before the war, customers had come into the shop to choose material, matching cottons and silks to embroider tablecloths. People made and mended their own clothes so buttons were needed. Almost everybody spent the long winter evenings sewing or knitting. I had always been intrigued as customers decided . . . this colour or that? When I grew up I resolved to run a haberdashery store.

In the meantime, Mamushia attempted to make the storeroom at the back of the shop as homely as possible.

Earlier, Zygmund had used the cart to help bring a small amount of furniture from the apartment. He helped Tatush cover the plain wood floor with an Indian carpet. Two mahogany bedsteads were placed in one corner and made up with mattresses and warm bedding. Finally, a large, mahogany wardrobe was set against the wall to hold everyone's clothes.

Since there was no kitchen, a small table by the back door held two gas rings with a few saucepans and plates by the side. Underneath the table, Mamushia had spread white paper over the bare floor and now used this to store potatoes, onions and bread. There was a tin for biscuits and one for tea. Butter and cheese where put into a box outside the door to keep cool. Everything was very cramped, but somehow Mamushia managed to make piping-hot soup and stews which we ate sitting on the bed.

Mamushia and Chucha spent time together every day, helping to eke out the stews and keeping each other as cheerful as possible.

The only entrance to the Ghetto was through an arched gateway in the white wall. Hundreds of families were now forced to live in this small area; every house overflowing with people having to share. Living conditions became very unhygienic.

There were very few lavatories in the houses and none in Ma Becky's place. The nearest one was the end of the shopping arcade and we always had to queue to use it. Otherwise, we used a pot.

A small square stood in the centre of the Ghetto with a few plane trees desolately clinging to life.

'Do you miss your trees, Grandfather?' I asked when I saw him.

'Well, of course I do,' he nodded. 'But come, look, I still have the Tree of Life.'

In his tiny room was his long, flat desk on which lay the Torah, the story of the Bible in Hebrew written on parchment and wound around wooden scrolls.

'Put your trust in the Almighty.'

He smiled tenderly and patted me on the head.

* * * * *

Summer 1940

One morning Tatush dressed and left our room early to try to organise some money with Mr Bombala. I sat on the edge of the bed watching Mamushia washing herself as best she could in the small, white china dish filled with warm water from the kettle. Suddenly I heard the clop of horses' hooves. I was sure I recognised the sound.

I quickly ran to the front of the shop, overjoyed to see Kasztan and Srebro outside, harnessed to the cart filled with provisions.

As Zygmund jumped down, I ran into his arms.

'I've brought you more food,' he beamed.

By the time Tatush returned, the sacks had been unloaded and stacked in the backyard.

Before Zygmund went on to see Grandfather he spent a long time talking to my father, shaking his head, tutting and nodding. He had gleaned news from his contacts in the timber trade about the atrocities taking place in other parts of Poland.

'The Nazis are not sending Jews for resettlement as they say, but to annihilate them. Whatever you do,' warned Zygmund, 'do not go on any of those transport trains.'

Stocks in both the bakers' and grocery shops were dwindling fast.

Early one summer dawn, Mamushia woke me up.

'Come on, we're going to queue for bread,' she said.

'Why do I have to come now?' I moaned.

'Because everyone else will be hoping to get some and I know there won't be enough for everybody.'

She put some money in my coat pocket.

'You wait by our local bakery and I'm going to the other shop by the square to queue there.'

By the time I arrived, the queue was already twenty people or so long. It was not until the sun was high in the sky that it started to move. At last, it was my turn.

'Children don't get loaves,' grumbled the sour shopkeeper, peering down at me.

'But I've been here for hours!' I cried, holding up the money.

The other shoppers confirmed this and she relented.

'Half a loaf then.'

She pulled the black, sticky bread apart, handed me half and I ran off, satisfied.

Eventually Mamushia appeared, carrying a loaf.

'These will have to last us for at least a week,' she said, carefully wrapping my half in brown paper and putting it on top of the wardrobe. All at once, outside, by the white wall, the sound of yelling and screaming made our hearts freeze. I ran to the shop door and saw young men being rounded up by grey-uniformed soldiers pointing guns at them. It was their wives and mothers who were making the noise.

Mamushia came and caught hold of me to pull me back, but not before I saw a soldier butt one of the women hard across her face, sending her flying to the ground. In that moment, I knew for certain we were at the mercy of an enemy, armed and vicious.

* * * * *

September 1940

By now, it was the Jewish New Year; Grandfather led prayers in his tiny room. His two brothers were there with him as well as my uncles, Mamushia's brothers. I squeezed in with my cousins to hear the singing. Several other men were there praying with us for better times. Somehow, I knew God could hear us and would help us.

There was good news at last. Jewish leaders in the Ghetto were informed by the Nazis that certain families could leave for Palestine.

'If only it were us!' exclaimed Mamushia.

Everyone felt uplifted. Freedom seemed very near.

Several weeks later, Grandfather was delighted to receive a letter from one family saying they were safely in Syria waiting to go into the Holy Land.

Then Grandfather came in, excited, to say that the Nazis offered a concession to professional Jews, doctors, professors, lawyers and rabbis. They, too, could leave with the families for Palestine if they wished.

'I'm only a poor businessman,' said Tatush, shrugging his shoulders.

There was much excitement as I watched them from the shop door, carrying their suitcases to the Ghetto gate to await transport. Friends and relatives kissed each other and hugged the children 'goodbye'.

'Aren't they lucky to be leaving?' I said to Ma Becky, who was squeezing my shoulder with her hand.

'Maybe it will be our turn next.'

She turned me back into the shop and closed the door.

When I went to see Grandfather in his room a few days later, I was astonished to find him weeping. I put my thin arms around his neck to comfort him. He shook his head, but said nothing and motioned me to go away.

Outside in the street, people were whispering, shaking their heads and falling silent in front of the children. It was only later, when I was playing with my buttons, unnoticed behind the counter, that I overheard Tatush talking to Ma Becky. I felt such horror that I could not breathe for fright.

'All of the, men, women and children,' he said, 'were driven straight from here to the cemetery, forced to dig their own graves and then shot.'

A terrified gloom fell over the people in the Ghetto matched only by the stench of overcrowding. Many more men were taken off by the German soldiers; it was said to dig trenches on the Russian front. Although everyone hoped and prayed the war would soon be over, things seemed to be getting worse very quickly.

*   *   *   *   *

December 1940

Now the Nazis decided to terrorise us. They ordered a squad of young soldiers to burst into the Ghetto streets firing automatic rifles at anybody around.

Ma Becky rushed to the front of the shop and pulled me safely back inside. We could hear the terrified screams of the wounded mixed with the laughter of the soldiers, enjoying the havoc and terror they had caused.

In the Ghetto, many people lay dead or bleeding. Soldiers pointed rifles at anyone left around and marched them towards the railway.

'Why? Why?' I sobbed into Ma Becky's bosom. 'What have we done wrong?'

But she had no answer either.

Next day an SS Officer with a loudspeaker declared in German: 'Achtung! Achtung! We will be moving people out, whether you want to go or not!'

Soldiers with rifles and dogs marched through the streets and came to a halt by the shopping arcade.

The loudspeaker shouted: 'You are to pack one suitcase each, take a loaf of bread for the journey and be ready to leave in half an hour.'

Once again, Ma Becky acted quickly.

As soon as she heard marching boots she called out to my parents, 'Make for the attic, quickly!'

Then she ran to the front and put up boarded shutters. Finally, she slammed and bolted the doors from the inside so that the shop looked closed and deserted.

'Don't make one sound,' she warned as she grabbed my hand and raced me upstairs to join the others.

The round, bedroom-attic window overlooked the station yard. From behind the dusty panes, my parents and I watched, horrified and silent, as hundreds of people were rounded up by German soldiers and made to board the first of the transport trains.

All of a sudden, I spotted two familiar figures amongst the crowd being herded along.

'There's Grandfather and Chucha!' I yelled. 'I want to go with them.'

Immediately, Tatush grabbed me from the window and clapped his hand over my mouth.

'How dare you? How dare you shout like that?' he hissed. 'Do you want to kill us all?'

Hours later, at dusk, an eerie silence closed in on the streets. In bed, Mamushia cuddled me tightly as we both cried for Grandfather and Chucha. I felt I might never see them again.

After that, Mamushia sobbed for hours on end as if her heart would break. She was inconsolable and nothing I could do made up for the loss of her dear father and sister.

The cruel, harsh winter remained with us. It was difficult to obtain any coal for heating and the weather was icy. In the mornings, we joined the queue of dozens of families waiting to use the one available toilet in the old shopping arcade. There was only one tap for fresh water nearby and Mamushia went to collect this in a jug each morning. She carefully rationed it, some for cooking and drinking and a tiny amount left lying all day in the white china basin for keeping my hands and face clean.

She wept often for Grandfather and Chucha, but her brother and sister-in-law were still nearby. My cousins, Jacob and Isaac, had already been taken with their family for transport, but my other cousins, Renia and Samuel and I kept ourselves warm on the natural skating rink in the square by attaching metal skates to our boots and playing together outside for hours.

As snow drifted onto the rooftops, everyone was losing hope of an early liberation. Tatush took me to one side to explain how he was going to get me out of the Ghetto.

'We are in great danger. You must understand, Goldie, living here with us is not safe.'

I looked very downcast.

He went on, 'My associate, Mr Bombala, has promised to do his utmost to save you. He is going to take you to a Mr and Mrs Niewski, who have offered to adopt you.'

I was horrified, but Tatush insisted I leave to stay with them, just to see if it would work.

Early next morning, he brought out a large, leather skin that could be made into shoes, which he tied around my thin body under my coat.

'This can be sold for money – give it to Mr Bombala. Make your way to our old apartment and he will look after you.'

No guards were at the open entrance. Tatush took me through and saw me on my way. Very reluctantly, I made my way to Zeromskiego 21, but before I could climb the stairs Mr

Bombala appeared at the entrance and guided me to another apartment; that of Mr and Mrs Niewski.

I remained outside the white walls with this kindly, childless couple for several weeks. Mr Niewski would play his piano to try to cheer me up, but I was so homesick and lonely for Mamushia that nothing they did helped. People could still move freely in and out of the Ghetto so I was able to visit her easily, but when I had to return to the Niewski's home, I could hardly bear the thought of leaving my family behind.

I did not have to for much longer. By the spring of 1941, the Nazis made a law that hiding or aiding Jews was punishable by death. We were to be hunted down like animals. It was going to be far too dangerous for Mr and Mrs Niewski to keep a Jewish child. They returned me to Mr Bombola.

As the door of Apartment 21 opened, Mrs Bombala ushered me quickly inside. It was strange to see other people there, not at all like going home – but they evidently expected me.

I was surprised to see Janina, from Mr Lipinski's shop, waiting in the sitting room. She smiled at me as Mr Bombala introduced her as his relative. Then he sat me down and tried to explain as best he could what was going to happen.

He looked at me intently.

'You will have to disappear.'

'I am going to try to make arrangements to take you to my sister in Warsaw,' said Janina, 'but you have to do one thing for me. You have to choose a new name. Will you do that for me?'

I nodded miserably. Not only was I about to leave Mamushia and Tatush, I was even losing my own name.

'It has to be a very Polish name,' advised Mr Bombala. 'What do you think you would like? Can you think of the name of any little Polish girl?'

My mind searched into the past. I tried to remember the happy days at school such a long time ago. I bit my lips together and then suddenly recalled the name of a classmate that I had liked.

'Can I be called Danuta Skalska?'

'Skalska, yes,' Mr Bombala agreed. 'Danuta, no. You should have a name beginning with G. Nearer to 'Goldie' then you will remember to react when you're called.'

He turned to Janina.

'What do you think?'

'Genoveve?' suggested Janina.

'No, shorter . . .' he thought. 'How about Genia? Goldie, would you like to be called Genia?'

I supposed so.

'Will you practice it to make sure you know it belongs to you?' asked Janina. 'Say it over and over to make sure?'

'Genia, Genia,' I repeated.

'That's right.' Mr Bombala patted me on the head. 'Now that's settled we can get you new papers. Goldie Rapaport is going to disappear. You will become Genia Skalska.'

Dusk was falling as Mr Bombala walked me back towards the Ghetto. Suddenly, from the park gates, came the sound of hysterical shrieking.

I spun round to see one of my old classmates standing pointing at me and screeching, 'Jewess! Jewess!' at the top of her voice.

The evil was uncontrollable. The whole world hated me and I could not understand why. I froze in terror.

Immediately, passersby ran to quieten the screaming child before any Germans could hear.

One of them slapped her round the face and hissed, 'Shut up!'

I stood, rigid with fright. My legs would not move then they began to give way under me. Mr Bombala quickly put his arms around me, lifted me up and carried me the rest of the way. Strangely, the Ghetto gates were open and he just carried me through to deliver me back safely.

In Mamushia's arms, I sobbed and clung to her in relief. I was not going to leave her ever again.

'I'll be in touch, though it may take some time,' whispered Mr Bombala as he moved away into the darkness.

*   *   *   *   *

Summer 1941

Nazi rules in the Ghetto became very severe. The arched gateway was closed permanently. No one was allowed out. Armed soldiers guarded the exit and, as the year wore on, food became almost unobtainable.

Not enough flour was available so it was mixed with wheat dust to make the black bread that was our main diet. There were hardly any vegetables and no fruit. No customers came to the corner shop. Zygmund was now unable to make contact and the stores he had brought were dwindling. We shared what we could with Ma Becky and her daughters who, in turn, shared their stocks of rice and barley.

Despite the increasingly harsh laws imposed by the Nazis, people still tried to keep life as normal as possible. Mamushia heard of an Argentinean lady who had started classes for little children.

'Would you like to go?'

Of course I would! I was taken to join eight children sitting on the floor around the teacher. For the first time in ages, I had something to think about.

The teacher held a slate on her lap and wrote words on it. I managed to bounce up and down shouting them out. We were very cramped in the tiny room, so every so often she would encourage us to stand and stretch out, pretending to be swaying trees. She taught us folk songs and made up a little play about how a garden grew. How proud I was when she picked me to be the cabbage!

As the year went on, I learnt to write sentences and read the small stock of children's books. I was growing taller and thinner. I always felt hungry and missed the cakes and buns from Mamushia's bakery. We all did.

I still attended the little schoolroom but we were very listless and some children did not turn up anymore.

One evening I overheard my uncle talking about the brave boys who were 'going over the wall' to bring back food for their families.

'Last night,' he said, 'a group got out – but some of them never came back.'

'Perhaps they have escaped,' said Mamushia hopefully.

'How far would they get? I don't think so.' My uncle looked desolate. 'We have no weapons now but prayer.'

* * * * *

Autumn 1941

Somehow we managed to hang on through the summer. As autumn approached, the days grew shorter. In the tiny square, the plane trees started shedding their leaves. A few birds still twittered in the branches.

The rounding up of Jews for transport began again in earnest. My teacher and all the people in her house disappeared overnight.

Then *'Achtung! Achtung!'* Soldiers were everywhere. This time Ma Becky was too slow boarding up the shop. She managed to put up one shutter before they grabbed her. She and her daughters were ordered into the street. The cases were already packed for 'transport' and since they obeyed orders to leave for the railway station, no one came looking around the shop or searched the storeroom at the back where the Rapaport family were hiding in terror.

After that, there was no sign of Germans in the Ghetto for a long while. They left nature to take its toll.

* * * * *

Winter closed in on us once more. Now people began to die of hunger. We had only one egg left, no bread and only a small store of vegetables. For the first time, I noticed how thin and drained Mamushia looked.

Her hair had turned grey, her gaunt face reflected great suffering and grief. She was only twenty-nine years old, but she looked completely worn out.

In the months since Grandfather and Chucha had been taken away, Mamushia seemed to lose her will to live. She lay on the bed for long stretches of time with her face to the wall, sobbing uncontrollably. I tried to bring comfort as best I could, patting her back, stroking her hair.

'Don't cry, my Mummy. We will soon see Grandfather again, you'll see,' I whispered, but Mamushia only shook her head and turned away.

Tatush went out, desperately trying to find food. Pangs of hunger gnawed at my stomach in painful cramps. I lay beside Mamushia sucking the corner of the blanket for comfort. I yearned to walk in the woods with Grandfather once more and return to his log cabin. Somehow, I knew that if I wanted to survive, then I would I have to leave the Ghetto, with or without my family.

4. ESCAPE

Spring 1942

Although all communication between the outside world and the inmates of the Ghetto was forbidden, true to their promise, somehow Mr Bombala, Janina and Tatush managed to lay plans together to save me.

'Will my cousins Renia and Samuel come too?' I wanted to know when I heard.

My father shook his head and tried to explain to me that it was impossible to protect Jewish boys like Samuel from the SS.

'And besides,' he said sadly of Renia, 'unlike you, she has dark hair and looks Jewish.'

My blonde hair and fair skin made me appear just like any other Polish child and I suppose that was why they could think of saving me without putting their whole family in jeopardy. It was just luck that Janina worked as housekeeper to Mr Lipinski in his grocery shop and that it backed on to the end of the shopping arcade where the lavatory was.

One other person was involved in the bid to save me from certain death. He was a Polish policeman called Izy, who had been a wood buyer for the large factory in Radom where firearms were made for local farmers and noblemen. I remember him coming to Grandfather's yard to choose mahogany for the silver-embossed handles of ceremonial pistols. In fact, once, long ago, he had presented me with a tiny replica gun which I kept and treasured. Now his factory had been taken over by the Germans and he had been compelled to join the police force and made to round up Jews for labour camps.

He must have remembered me with affection and although there was little he could do against the might of the armed and evil invaders, he was determined to do what he could to hoodwink the enemy.

Tatush tried as best he could to prepare me for my new life. One evening he sat me on the edge of the bed and knelt in front of me, holding my hands firmly in his.

'You are going away from us for a while to stay with a family with three children, just to be safe.'

I nodded miserably.

'You must be a good girl, listen and obey and do not cause any extra work and help out in the house all you can.'

Tiny tears trickled down the side of my nose which I tried to sniff back. Tatush put his finger to my cheek.

'One day I will come and get you,' he said softly. 'I promise,' and he lifted me down from the bed.

As the sky turned dark outside, Tatush wrapped me in my warm, brown coat and placed a meagre pile of clothes into a bag. In his own pocket he had slipped a screwdriver and a small leather pouch.

'Now, say goodbye to Mummy.'

He pushed me firmly towards Mamushia who had watched silently, standing by the door, with a look of anguish on her face. When I reached her, she tenderly smoothed my hair with both hands then bent to hug me.

I entwined my thin, little arms tightly around her neck whilst she held on to me whispering, 'Please God, you will be safe.'

Tatush gently prised me away from my darling Mamushia.

'Don't upset the child,' he said softly.

He opened the door to the backyard and took my hand. Mamushia's arms stretched out towards me as we parted. I could hear her stifled sobs as Tatush led me into the street. Tears stung behind my eyes as I was hurried along.

'If anyone stops us we will say we are going to the toilet inside the arcade,' he whispered.

The shopping arcade was boarded up at one end where it joined the back of Mr Lipinski's shop. The white, notched planks were roughly nailed together. Tatush made sure that no one was around before he carefully prised open three boards and removed them as quietly as he could.

The gap revealed the back window of the grocer's shop. He knocked on the pane . . . tap-tap, tap-tap-tap . . . a prearranged signal.

There was the sound of the window opening inwards. Tatush bent down to life me up and whispered, 'Be good. See you soon.'

Two hands came out from the window and grasped me under the arms as Tatush hoisted me up. I was hauled in over the sill and set down in a very dark room. The bag was handed up after me. My heart sank as I heard the window being quickly shut and the sound of the boards being replaced.

'This is my bedroom,' whispered Janina. She lit a small lamp by one of the beds. 'Come now, to sleep and we will travel to Warsaw tomorrow.'

Gently she undressed me and tucked me under the blankets. Janina was not married and was too old to have children, but she was full of compassion for me.

I tried to be good, but now that Tatush had gone and Mamushia was not there, I could not help crying. I lay for a long time sobbing into the pillow until, despite my misery, I fell into a sound sleep.

When I awoke the next morning there was no one in the room. As I gradually came to, I found that I was lying on a cold and clammy patch of bedding. I was horrified to realise I had wet the bed. I was far too ashamed to admit it and terrified of what Janina would do.

Just then Janina bustled into the room with some hot milk.

'Come along, sleepy head,' she smiled. 'Time to get up.'

But I shook my head. I did not dare to get up. I lay with my face peeping over the sheet and every time Janina said, 'Come on!' I shook my head and refused to move.

What would Janina do when she knew the truth? But I could not stop her putting her hands into the bed to lift me out.

31

As soon as she discovered the accident, all she said was, 'Never mind, my love. It is because you're alone and afraid – and missing your mummy. Let's wash the sheets together, shall we?'

Janina was so kind and tender that, to my relief, everything was all right. By the end of the morning, she had explained to me what was going to happen.

'You can't stay in Radom because all your classmates know you. You will be much safer a long way away from here. This afternoon I am going to take you to stay with my sister in Warsaw. She is kind and willing to have you stay for as long as the war lasts . . . you will be her little niece.'

I suddenly felt a great rush of love for her kindness and courage because I realised that in doing all this Janina, herself, was going to be in great danger.

Just after two o'clock, Izy, the Polish policeman, entered Mr Lipinski's grocery shop and came through to the back premises. I shivered with fear as he spelt out to us the danger in trying to help a Jewish child escape the Gestapo.

'If the SS stop you because they know you are Jewish,' he said to me, 'you must not deny it. You will have to go with them. I will say that I spotted you and arrested you.'

He turned to Janina.

'You can either say you were walking out with me when I arrested her or you can say you know her and were trying to help her escape. Then you will have to bear the consequences. It will be death for both of you.'

'Hardly a choice,' snorted Janina. 'Well, I want to get it over with as quickly as possible. Let's go!'

As we put on our coats, Janina took a headscarf from her pocket and tied it over my head, pulling it forward to hide my face as much as possible.

Then we gathered our bags together and set off for the station. The moment she stepped onto the street, Janina made the sign of the cross and murmured a prayer.

She held my hand tightly as we walked on the pavement beside Izy. Trams trundled past and German vehicles were everywhere. Every single minute, around every corner, I thought someone would recognise me and start screaming again. I kept my head bent right down and watched my feet, but this time no one did.

At the station, Janina and I hung back while Izy bought tickets. We boarded a stationary train already packed with passengers, nobody speaking to anyone else.

There was space for three further down the train and we squeezed in just as guards came through the carriages inspecting identity papers.

Izy nonchalantly took papers from the inside pocket of his uniform and make a joke with the guard who hardly glanced at them before handing them straight back. I let my breath out, but suddenly my heart seemed to stop as we heard yells and screams coming from the next carriage.

Through the window, I saw several people being herded along the platform at gunpoint. Seconds later, the whistle blew and the train jerked to life. It moved slowly forward, getting up speed until it had gathered speed to take me from the only town I had ever known towards the capital city of Poland, Warsaw.

Janina sat, looking tense and worried. She had put me nearest the window and when another guard passed she deliberately took hold of my gold plaits pretending to retie the ribbon.

The train pulled into several stations along the line where there was hustle and bustle as passengers dismounted or boarded. At every stop more soldiers came through the carriages to check papers. Janina's hands clenched so tightly as they approached that her knuckles went white. Oddly enough, I suppose because Izy was in uniform and appeared to be on official business, they just nodded at him and passed on.

I had never been on such a journey before. The rides on the cart with Grandfather had been calm and leisurely. Now I sat by the window next to Janina, our backs to the engine, jolting and

33

swaying to the motion of the carriage. I watched the flat fields and forests of Poland hurry by, taking me farther away from home than I had ever been.

Smoke drifted past in white patches from the front of the train. The rhythmic chugging of the engine, with the sound of wheels on the track, lulled me into a dreamland. I was with Grandfather once again, running through the forest with the warm sun on my face, trying to catch butterflies. I was brought back to reality when Janina rummaged around in her bag and handed me a carrot to chew.

After nearly two hours journeying, at the one stop before Warsaw, Izy whispered something to Janina, squeezed her hand and then stood up and left us. He intended to return to Radom before he was missed. I don't know how I stopped myself from running after him.

I wanted to go home.

5. WARSAW

We arrived at Warsaw Central Station in the evening when it was dark. People were milling around on their way home from work. Single-decker trams ran noisily on rails along the streets. Even in wartime, I was overwhelmed by the city twinkling with lights. The buildings were grander than any I had seen in my whole life.

I held close to Janina, frightened to lose contact with the only person I knew. We boarded a tram going towards the district of Praga, and stood at the back until we were able to squeeze into one seat just before the tram crossed over the Kerbedzie Bridge.

Finally, after half an hour or so, Janina indicated it was the stop to alight. She helped me hop down and we walked the last part of the journey towards Jagellonska 32.

Towering above me was a great, green, iron gate, shut to the outside. Janina pulled the bell and a bearded Janitor peered through the patterned top, recognised her and let us through the passageway into the first courtyard. Three storeys of blank windows rose like a forbidding fortress. I was hurried past into the back courtyard then in through a wooden door and up wooden stairs to the third floor.

My legs ached as we climbed to the top where Janina knocked on the door of Flat 32. The door was immediately opened and she led me into her sister's apartment.

The front entrance opened into a large, well-lit hall, elegantly carpeted and surrounded by many doors. The walls were decorated with framed pictures and it all seemed much grander than Flat 21 in Radom.

Later, I learned that the Grudzinski family had been well off and were all well educated. Mr Grudzinski had been a lecturer and teacher, but like everyone else in Poland, their circumstances changed for the worse as the war progressed.

Janina and her sister, Zofia Grudzinski, hugged and kissed each other whilst I stood silently, staring around.

'This is little Genia Skalska,' said Janina, emphasising my new name.

I managed to glance into Mrs Grudzinski's compassionate face, but I was so tired and drained that I could not respond in any way.

She held out her hand to me.

'Come, Genia, let me look at my little niece,' she said, but I did not move.

By now I stood with my eyes downcast and would not look up. Zofia bent down and put her arm around my shoulder.

'I am your Aunt Zofia.' She smiled at me. 'Come.'

She led me into a huge, elegant living room. It was filled with bookcases, pictures, icons, and ornaments. Around the large dining table, which was covered with a lace cloth, sat several people. As I was shown gently into the room, all heads turned and everyone stared at me.

A good-looking, young man of about eighteen put down the book he was reading and studied me with intense eyes.

'Hello!' he greeted me cheerfully.

'This is your cousin Stefan,' said my new 'aunt'. 'He is studying chemistry.'

I did not respond.

'And this is my daughter, your cousin Zoshienka, who works in Warsaw.'

A beautiful, young lady in her early twenties, with long, dark hair and blue eyes, looked up and smiled encouragingly. She was busy at the table making fancy little celluloid baskets in which to keep trinkets.

A girl, older than me, with a moon-shaped face and bright eyes, sat next to her sister watching me with a look of fear on her face. I half expected her to start screaming 'Jewess!' at me, but she was silent.

'This is your cousin Mira,' went on Mrs Grudzinski, 'and here is your Uncle Leon Grudzinski.'

It was all becoming too much to take in. I stood still and uncommunicative, staring at the floor. I did not want new uncles or aunts or cousins. I just wanted Mamushia and Tatush, or Grandfather and Chucha.

I felt a hand placed gently under my chin as she attempted to lift up my drooping head.

'Come, don't look so solemn,' she whispered.

But it was no use. I was too upset to do anything except burst into tears.

As I sobbed uncontrollably, this wonderful lady enveloped me against her ample figure and caressed my head, crooning, 'Don't cry, sweetheart. We are your family. We will look after you.'

But nothing seemed to staunch the flow of my despair. Mira got down from the table and silently put out her hand, but it was refused and my sobbing continued. I could not stop crying even if I had wanted to. Nothing anyone could do or say would pacify me.

All at once, Zoshienka rose from the table and placed one of the delicate little baskets into my hands.

'Do you like this?' she said. 'You can have it. It's yours.'

I looked down at the tiny, trim basket. I had never seen anything so pretty. I was so taken aback I stopped crying immediately.

'Come and sit with your family at the table,' encouraged Stefan, patting the chair beside him.

But that was too much for me and I shook my head resolutely. I stood quite still, clutching the basket, my lips pursed, eyes downcast. Kind as they were, I did not want to be part of that family at all.

Mr Grudzinski studied me with his kindly, deep-set, brown eyes. He was about fifty, with greying hair and yellow teeth, an intelligent and compassionate man who had lectured in history at Warsaw University. He was well aware of the tyranny outside that was changing the course of Poland's future.

He, too, was being hounded by the Nazis, who had made his life intolerable by imposing restrictions on teaching. I discovered later that he now spent his time looking after children in the poorer area of Warsaw.

'We must leave the child alone to settle down,' he said.

All the while, Janina had been watching and coaxing me to behave, but now, exasperated by my lack of co-operation, she declared sternly, 'Well, if you don't like it here I can take you back to the Ghetto.'

That was exactly what I wanted.

'All right,' I said, brightening up immediately.

'Tomorrow morning then, we will go back to where you came from,' Janina announced sharply and followed Zofia into the kitchen.

I sighed with relief and fondled the gift in my hands. Then I smiled briefly at Mr Grudzinski who winked back at me. He left the dining table and walked over to a long, tall desk upon which many books were stacked. He searched through them to pick out a small picture book.

'Will you listen if I read aloud to you?' he asked, opening his eyes wide and smiling with his big, yellow teeth.

I nodded as he sat himself down in an armchair.

'I am going to read very quietly, so you will have to come nearer. Will you come and sit on my lap?'

I shook my head.

'Well, come sit on the arm of my chair,' he coaxed.

Despite myself, I instinctively felt drawn to this strange, kindly man. He had the same ways about him as Grandfather. It was a quality that made me want to be close to him.

As he started to read softly, I edged towards him, leaning against the armchair the better to hear his calm voice.

I remember he related the story of a little red car on its travels; how a small girl and her brother had adventures in it and, as he read, I became transported away into the fairyland of the book.

I lost all sense of time, wanting him to go on to the happy ending. When it finished he placed the book on his knee and stroked my cheek.

'You see, we've finished the story while Auntie has been busy,' he said, pointing to the table which was now laden with food. 'Let's eat now and I'll read you another one afterwards.'

The food on the table was nothing like I had ever seen before. Thick chunks of greasy, dark red sausage wurst, cooked in cabbage-like sauerkraut, was served out and everyone immediately set to it with spoon and fork. All except me.

'It looks and smells disgusting,' I thought, sitting with my hands in my lap, staring at the plate.

Stefan eyed my portion hungrily.

'If she doesn't want it, I'll eat it,' he said.

I was astonished. No one had ever asked to take food from me before, but I lifted the plate and handed it over to him.

Afterwards there was bread and dripping, or jam if you wanted something sweet. I still refused to eat anything. Somewhere at the back of my mind was a strict rule that persuaded me not to eat unkoshered food, no matter how hungry I was.

However, I did drink some tea. Strong, black tea like Mamushia had ordered in the café in Radom, carefully placing a lump of sugar on my tongue, like the Russians, before I drank it.

Afterwards, whilst the family helped to clear away, 'Uncle Leon' took me over to his very own armchair again.

'We won't read any more,' he said. 'Instead, I'll teach you to play a game.'

From a drawer in the long book table he produced a wooden box which opened to reveal small, oblong pieces. Despite myself, I was curious.

'These are dominoes,' he said as they clattered out on to the table, black or white side up. 'Look at the dots, you can make numbers with them,' he explained. 'So let's see if you can find a six.'

You would have thought that by now I would have been so exhausted that my mind would not grasp anything new, but I was so overwrought and tense that searching for numbers in the dots was just the thing to calm my racing brain. For a time I forgot the upheavals of the past and began to enjoy myself.

After the game, which somehow Uncle Leon had allowed me to win, I helped replace the dominoes in their box.

'These are not made of wood,' I realised, recalling Grandfather's lessons.

'No. They're ivory, just like the keys on my piano, but we've had to sell that recently.'

He sounded sad.

'Can you really play a piano?'

No one that I knew was musical. His deep laugh enchanted me.

'Let me hum you Brahms's Lullaby,' he offered.

I drew nearer, leaning against him, the tune going round and round in my m mind, gradually drifting into sleep.

'Now it's time for bed,' said Uncle Leon.

Zoshienka took me into her bedroom where I settled down calmly in a strange bed in an unfamiliar city, happy to feel safe and knowing that I would be going back to Radom next day.

6. THE CHURCH

When I awoke next morning, I was upset to find Janina had already left. But Tatush had been insistent that I be as little trouble as possible, so I sighed, but said nothing.

Zoshienka and Stefan were not there either, and Mira was getting ready to go with her father to school. She left without even looking at me. I suppose she was astute enough to realise that my presence was putting her family in great danger.

'You must stay here with me,' her mother told me.

Mrs Grudzinski was much stouter and older than Mamushia. Grey hair framed her homely face and huge, blue eyes looked candidly at the troubled world. She seemed to have the same quality of openness and endurance as Zygmund.

'Call me 'Aunt Zofia' – you can, can't you?' she encouraged.

I tried to be as helpful as I could in the apartment where everything was clean and tidy. By the end of the week, I began to feel much safer with 'Aunt Zofia' and her family. But Mira was very suspicious of me.

Eventually, one evening in the kitchen, she said, 'You're Jewish, aren't you?'

I did not say a word, but pretended to tidy up.

'Down the road there used to be a Jewish school. Now it is empty and neglected. No one is allowed to go near.' She peered at my white face. 'There's something dangerous about being Jewish, isn't there?'

There was, but I did not know why.

Aunt Zofia heard as she bustled in with the plates and placed a warning finger on her lips.

Early one Sunday morning, while Zoshienka and I were still in our beds asleep, Aunt Zofia came hurrying in with Mira behind her.

'Come, we are going to church,' she announced. 'I have something for you, Genia.'

41

As I jumped out of bed, she placed in my hand a silver chain on which brown and white beads were strung at intervals. It was like a necklace with a small cross at the bottom.

'Look, this white bead alone is the Our Father,' Mira showed me.

'Do you know Our Father?' asked Aunt Zofia looking intently at me.

I shook my head dumbly. Was Uncle Leon our father?

'Well, Mira and I will teach it to you.'

'The brown beads are Hail Marys,' said Mira knowingly.

'Hail Mary, full of grace, the Lord is with you. Blessed be thy name and blessed be the fruit of thy womb, Jesus,' Mira intoned.

At the word 'Jesus' I started to shake and cry.

'Why, darling, whatever is the matter?' Aunt Zofia's arms were suddenly around me.

'I didn't kill him, I didn't!' I sobbed.

'No, of course you didn't,' soothed Aunt Zofia.

'The headmaster said I did,' I went on, with all the suppressed words tumbling out. 'He made all the Jewish children stand up in class and said we killed Jesus and everyone should hate us. And then they started to throw things and a rubber hit my eye. I never killed Jesus. I've never killed anything. I don't even know Jesus!'

I was hysterical.

Aunt Zofia kept cuddling me and then said softly, 'Dry your eyes, little one. Jesus is kind. He will save us all. Come, dress quickly, I'm taking you to church.'

Before breakfast, we left the apartment. Aunt Zofia walked briskly in front with Zoshienka, while Mira and I followed. The red and white brick church with the tall spires was just around the corner. It was named St Floriana, after the patron saint of firemen.

As we made our way through the entrance I saw, in an alcove to the left, a huge, white statue of a man on a cross. I gasped. His hands and feet were nailed to the wood. On his head was a crown of thorns. His eyes were half-open in agony. I was compelled to stare at him, but strangely, his lips seemed to smile at me as I drew near. He seemed so real I suddenly felt that if I talked to him he would answer back. Somehow I knew this was Jesus, but he was not angry with me and I was not afraid.

On entering the main church, I watched Mira dip her fingers into a stone bowl filled with holy water.

'Do what I do,' she whispered, so I copied her and knelt beside her on the stone floor trying to make the sign of the cross.

The church inside reminded me of Grandfather's synagogue with rows of polished, wooden pews. But this church was much larger, with alcoves along the sides containing statues and icons. High above, beautiful, stained glass windows filtered light on to the altar. All was serene. People sat quietly or knelt in prayer as an organ above the nave played softly.

'Sometimes I sing up there.'

Mira pointed to the balcony high above the transept

At the far end I could see a priest holding a goblet.

'He's taking Mass,' whispered Mira, but I could not understand any of the Latin words or what was happening.

Choirboys and officiates, dressed in white robes, knelt at the rails of the altar to take the sacrament and as each rose, they too, made the sign of a cross.

'Kneel and say Our Father after me,' said Aunt Zofia quietly when we reached the pews.

So I repeated the words of the prayer, feeling they were familiar, seeming in some way to reflect the holy books Grandfather read.

'Our Father, which art in Heaven,
Hallowed be Thy Name,
Thy Kingdom come,
Thy Will be done, on Earth as it is in Heaven.
Give us this day our daily bread,
And forgive us our trespasses . . .'

43

It seemed like a Jewish prayer . . . 'for this and all our sins, forgive us, Lord.'

After the service, Zoshienka showed me a side altar with the impressive icon of the Black Madonna encrusted with jewels and decorated with necklaces. Several women in earnest prayer knelt before her, counting their rosary beads.

Zoshienka told us she was staying to speak with the priest, Father Yuri and that we should walk on home without her. I was silent on the way back, quite overawed by my experience in church.

'Do you like our church?' Uncle Leon enquired later.

'Oh, yes I do!' I breathed. 'Who is the statue outside of the lady holding a baby?'

'Don't you know anything?' Mira snorted. 'That's Hail Mary.'

'That is Our Lady, Queen of Poland, mother of Jesus Christ,' said Aunt Zofia.

'She's very beautiful,' I said. 'She looks like Mamushia.'

Tears traced down my face.

'Come now,' encouraged Aunt Zofia, 'I've heard from Janina. Your parents are both happy you're with us. That's good isn't it?'

*   *   *   *   *

Christmas 1942

On Christmas Eve, I was taken to join hundreds of people at St Floriana's for midnight mass.

A huge Christmas tree stood at one side of the nave, decorated with baubles and many coloured candles. It was a night of magic and mystery, listening to the carols and seeing the crib with the Holy Family and the Wise Men all alight with twinkling white lights.

'Why does the baby have a ring round his head?' I wanted to know.

'That is the baby Jesus and the halo shows His Glory,' said Aunt Zofia. 'He is God and He is good. Pray to Him and He will help you.'

'Pray to Our Lady,' added Mira, 'Holy Mother of God to intercede for you.'

I had no idea what she meant, but that night I prayed as hard as I could to the baby in the manger – to let me be with Mamushia once again.

One afternoon, soon after Christmas, as the family sat together in the living room, a knock at the door made us all jump. Stefan answered the door and I was overjoyed to see Janina, paying one of her rare visits to Warsaw.

I quite forgot the deadly peril I was in and raced over to grab her hand, crying, 'Have you seen Mamushia and Tatush? Am I going home today?'

'No!'

Janina angrily pushed me away. I was aghast.

'You must never mention them again – ever. Do you hear?' she hissed.

She hastily left the room beckoning Aunt Zofia to follow.

I walked desolately into the bedroom. My only link with home was here in the apartment and I was not allowed to talk about it. Everything that I loved and remembered was forbidden. I lay on the top of the bed, sobbing, in a fog of sadness and despair.

7. THE RESISTANCE

Spring 1943

Although I did my best to settle into my new life, I watched Mira skip to school wishing I could go as well. Instead, Aunt Zofia read with me or set me some writing. When Uncle Leon was there, he taught me simple arithmetic or we played dominoes.

Every now and again, parcels of food arrived on the doorstep from relatives in the country.

'Perhaps it is from Zygmund,' I thought.

Whenever there was a knock at the door someone would hiss at me, 'Quickly, into the back room!' and I would have to scamper out of sight.

This time it was Father Yuri, the handsome, clean-shaven priest at St Floriana's who had arrived to speak with Zoshienka.

'It's all right, you can come back!' she called out.

Zoshienka and Stefan had joined the underground resistance and attended regular meetings and briefings. Father Yuri was one of their contacts.

Another young man named Zbyszek often called to collect Stefan on the way to their local underground meetings and I was allowed to see him too.

He noticed me standing there, small and quiet.

'Hello, who are you?' he asked, bending down to look at me.

'I'm . . .' I faltered. 'I'm Genia Skalska, that's who I am!'

I spoke in my purest Polish accent and flashed my eyes, daring him to say otherwise. He grinned at me and turned away.

I heard him mutter to Stefan, 'How can those bloody Nazis want to murder children like this?'

He suddenly looked mad with anger.

There was just one more young man I was allowed to see and that was Sebastian Kalwasinski. Such a handsome fellow! I wanted to know all about him and Zoshienka confided in me that he was courting her, but she was troubled since he had just been called to join the Navy.

I imagined he was as gallant as any sailor could be. She was captivated by his jaunty air and so was I.

When her sweetheart knocked on the door, Zoshienka laughed gaily, 'That's my Sebastian!'

She ran to let him in, tossing back her long, wavy hair. There he would stand, flowers in hand, ready to take her out. Her retrousse nose wrinkled delightfully as she beamed up at him. I felt quite jealous. He was such fun to be with, but since I was only eight and Zoshienka was twenty-one . . .

She was truly beautiful with a heart-shaped face. Kindness and good humour shone from her large, luminous eyes. When I grew up I wanted to have a perfect figure with a tiny waist just like Zoshienka. When she wore her best platform shoes, her tight jacket with padded shoulders and her knee-length skirt she looked stunning.

If Zoshienka was not ready, Sebastian came into the sitting room and amused Mira and me with funny tales. We sat, wide-eyed, eagerly taking it all in.

'Isn't he wonderful?' breathed Mira as he led her sister out of the door.

'Yes, he is!' I sighed.

Mira loved him because, she told me, he had the happy knack of turning up by the school playground to take her off for an ice cream.

We both thought Zoshienka the luckiest girl alive, but not all visitors were trustworthy.

One evening, as the family sat around the table with black tea and black bread there was loud banging on the door. Stefan jumped up and quickly pushed me into the bedroom. Fear caught at my throat. Had the SS come for me?

'Stay put and don't make one sound,' he whispered through his teeth.

I slid under the bed, cowed and trembling. It was such a long wait I became quite numb with cold.

Eventually I dared to creep out to snuggle under the bedcovers and fall fast asleep.

I was woken by voices muttering outside the bedroom, 'It's so dangerous having her here!'

All my fears rose inside me. Everything was uncertain for me. My family was miles away, but here, in Warsaw, I had really begun to love Aunt Zofia and her family. I did not want to jeopardise them and felt very upset. I lay awake for a long time after that, wondering what I could do to make it up to them.

As the war dragged on the family somehow managed to be together intermittently. Sebastian was no longer around courting Zoshienka. He had been conscripted into the German Navy.

Stefan was in the underground movement that worked day and night to disrupt the German occupation of our country. Aunt Zofia and Uncle Leon were constantly worried about him, especially when word came through that Army machinery had been attacked and railways blown up.

They smiled with relief the minute he arrived home. He always gave Mira and me a hug, then sat down to eat with gusto. He laughingly told Uncle Leon that, because they were short of funds, he had had to hold up a bank and wasn't at all surprised when the cashiers were delighted to hand over the money. It was all in a good cause.

Occasionally, news from outside Poland filtered through. Some was good news that Stefan repeated eagerly to the family in the evenings around the table.

'The allies are advancing. One day the Russians will come from the east; British and Americans will make a push from the west. We are to hold on and be ready to rise against the Nazis when our time comes.'

He was eventually fully occupied as leader of a special underground group 'Agat', whose headquarters were in Krakow then we hardly saw him.

Zoshienka's beauty was a great asset to the Resistance. I suspected she made a splendid decoy. Her daily outings were to an office in the centre of the city, but she could not always have been engaged in office work because, occasionally, like Stefan, she was away for several nights.

She would return looking exhausted and flop on to her bed, fully clothed, to sleep. When she woke, Aunt Zofia fussed over her with steaming chicory tea or hot soup set to one side for her.

No one ever questioned where she had been, but when her bed was empty we were all tense and worried until she returned safe and sound.

One evening, after Easter, Mira called me to the window.

'Look at the colour of the sky,' she said, pointing to the curious glow over the rooftops.

'Why are there such black clouds?' I wondered.

'I don't know, but I think something is burning.'

We two girls watched as the clouds of smoke drifted over the district of Praga. That night Stefan and Zbyszek appeared, dirty and worn out. Both slept exhaustedly in Stefan's room. Later, I discovered that the Warsaw Ghetto inmates had made one last stand against the horror of Nazism.

Almost starved to death and seeing their loved ones rounded up for transport to the gas chambers, they had managed, with the help of the Resistance, to get hold of weapons. In a last-ditch stand they had challenged the mighty Germans.

Zbyszek, with others, had managed to escape. Now the whole area of the Ghetto was being burnt to the ground in revenge.

* * * * *

In Warsaw, food was becoming extremely scarce. Mira got a meal at school, but I always had hunger gnawing inside me.

Uncle Leon managed a small allotment nearby to grow vegetables for the kitchen, but in spring the crops were meagre.

'I've nothing to cook but radishes,' Aunt Zofia moaned. 'Food on the Black Market is so expensive. We shall have to sell something.'

She tried several times to sell antiques, but who wanted such things when the people of Poland were beginning to starve?

Then, miraculously, she managed to get word to relations way out on a farm and once more small parcels of butter, cheese or clotted cream arrived on the doorstep.

Mira was at school when the first parcel of bright yellow butter was delivered. Aunt Zofia gave me a delighted cuddle.

'I'm going to eke this out, but first . . .' She cut a crust of bread, spreading the soft butter on it. 'This is for you. Isn't this a treat?'

'It's delicious!' I agreed, sucking the bread slowly, trying to keep the taste in my mouth for as long as possible.

When the next batch of farm produce arrived, Aunt Zofia decided to sell part of it.

'Now is your chance to help with the war effort. We are going to pat this butter flat, like a book, see?'

She wrapped the butter in brown paper and then sandwiched it between two books.

'That doesn't look suspicious, does it?' she asked. 'Now, you take this to the Janitor and see what he does.'

I half ran down the wooden stairs and out into the courtyards.

When I came upon the Janitor in his room, I held out the parcel saying, 'My Auntie wants you to have this.'

'What?'

He rose from his table curiously.

'Ah, the little girl from the country. Well, what have we here?'

He discounted the books immediately and his eyes lit up at the yellow butter. He rummaged around in a drawer and produced several zloties which he jingled into my hands. I was holding money!

I grabbed back the books and skipped all the way back through the courtyards and up the stairs, flushed and excited from my errand, to hand the money to Aunt Zofia. She hugged me tightly.

'At last,' I thought, 'I can be of some use.'

* * * * *

One evening, after a visit from Father Yuri, Zoshienka said cautiously, 'I have promised Dr Zill that he will have butter tomorrow.'

She slipped a piece of paper with an address on it into her mother's apron pocket. Aunt Zofia looked startled.

'I know. It's too dangerous for you to go,' Zoshienka agreed, 'but children will be ignored. Send Genia and Mira after school and tell them to return to the church for evensong.'

She was giving the commands.

Next afternoon, when Mira returned, a butter pat lay already wrapped in brown paper and tied between two books. Aunt Zofia spread open a map of Warsaw on the kitchen table and traced her finger along the river until she came to the Kerbedzie Bridge then over it and into the city centre.

'Look,' she showed us. 'If you take the tram to here and then walk along this street, you will come to number 21, the surgery of Dr Zill. Knock this special knock . . .' she rapped the sign on the table, 'then hand over the butter. Don't talk to anyone on the way – not even to each other. And take your rosaries to say on the tram. When you've delivered the butter, ask for the money and then return straight to our church.'

'This is going to be our adventure,' said Mira delightedly, but I felt very fearful.

It was the middle of the afternoon when we set off with the parcel. We soon caught a tram and found seats. Mira sat twiddling her rosary beads and mouthing Hail Marys. I clutched my beads and stared out the window as the tram trundled along.

My heart jumped in panic as I saw German troops everywhere. Some even boarded the tram, but Zoshienka was right, no one took any notice of two little girls with black and red rose-patterned, Polish headscarves tied tightly over their flaxen plaits, both evidently going to church.

When we alighted, I followed on behind Mira. She found the doctor's flat easily.

First, she gave the special knock on the door. When the doctor's wife appeared, we were hurriedly let in, past the doctor's surgery, where I was horrified to see German officers in the waiting room.

Once safely inside the kitchen, the doctor's wife opened our parcel and took out the butter.

'How much?' she asked.

I don't know why, but I immediately said, '25 zloties.'

The money was counted out without question and handed to Mira, who put it in her coat pocket.

'You will go straight to church now,' said the doctor's wife, 'but first . . .'

She turned to the dresser, opened her sewing box and took out two ornate hatpins and two pieces of paper. Carefully, she placed a piece of paper inside my blouse and fastened it on the outside with a hatpin. She did the same to Mira.

Then she rearranged our headscarves so that the pins where hidden, patted us on our cheeks and hurried us out into the street.

By the time we boarded the tram home, it was almost dusk and the light had completely gone as we approached St Floriana's.

When we entered, the church was glowing with candles. I suddenly had an overwhelming longing for Mamushia and home. Instead of an elderly woman lighting a candle in front of the Madonna, I imagined Mamushia with her hands covering her eyes, praying over the Sabbath candles; I could hear Grandfather reciting blessings over the wine and bread; I saw Tatush wrapped in his prayer shawl.

I knelt beside Mira and sobbed in spasms for my short, secure past. Mira said her rosary and pretended not to notice.

When evensong was over and the church almost empty, Father Yuri came down the aisle towards the back pews. He wore a long, black cassock with a silver and gold scarf. A large cross hung from his belt. He stopped, bent over us making the sign of the cross, unpinned the messages from our blouses, slipped them into his cassock then he hurried on.

From then on, many times Mira and I delivered butter or cheese to the doctor's surgery for money, collected messages from him and carried these to the church. We knew this was how the Resistance worked and it was a very dangerous thing to do. But it was adventurous and exciting being on important missions. Somehow, we never counted the consequences.

Father Yuri, however, was especially cautious when a stranger was in church. He walked quickly past us as we knelt and turned into the confessional box.

We waited to see if anyone went in and if it was all clear, Mira took in the messages while I prayed as hard as I could to Jesus to help us.

Mrs Grudzinski always waited anxiously for us to return safely.

'I got 27 zloties for the butter this time!' I glowed, pleased with myself for putting up the price and being able to help a little.

I knew very well that the money was important for our survival.

* * * * *

Autumn 1943

The war continued. Parcels from the country stopped arriving and the mainstay meal of the family became a ration of brown flour soaked overnight in water then stirred over a very low flame. The longer Aunt Zofia cooked it, throwing in bits of carrot or onion, the thicker it became.

'Yuk! It tastes like glue!' I thought, but I kept quiet because it lined my stomach and staved off hunger pains. Going to bed hungry was the hardest thing.

'Please can we have some real bread tonight? I'm so hungry,' I begged.

'I have a kind of sweet for you,' said Aunt Zofia.

She opened her button box and selected some large, white, pearl buttons, just like Ma Becky used to sell.

'Pop one into your mouth – don't swallow – but suck it like a boiled sweet. Imagine it is something delicious.'

She handed one to Mira as well and put one in her own mouth, sucking with loud noises.

Strangely enough, this trick worked. All three of us sat around imagining we were sucking the most delicious sweets.

'Just like sugar lumps,' I said.

'Mine is like minty barleys,' said Mira.

'Mine is a peppermint,' said Aunt Zofia.

*   *   *   *   *

Bleak days followed as the thermometer dropped and the wind howled outside, tossing away the last of the leaves of the plane trees in Jagellonska. There was never enough fuel for heat all day and the flat was icy cold.

Stefan and Zoshienka were rarely in the apartment and neither was Uncle Leon. I lay snuggled down under my bedcovers, unwilling to get dressed in the shivering cold that made my teeth chatter.

Aunt Zofia bustled in and jostled me out of bed.

'Come on, lazy head, exercise will do you good!'

She flung her arms wide and bent her knees for demonstration. I could not help giggling as I got dressed.

'Get warm!' she insisted. 'Help me beat the mattresses with straw beaters.'

So Mira and I set to, keeping up a steady beat until we felt warm enough to sit in our coats, wrapped around with eiderdowns, our faces just peeping out, while Aunt Zofia told us stories of her childhood and how young ladies should behave.

When we had sat long enough, she would brisk about saying, 'Come along, now we have the dusting to do – but like this . . . jump!' and we jumped and ran around with dusters, just to keep warm.

Somehow we lived through the long winter until the plane trees along the street started to produce their light green buds.

'Spring always brings a sense of hope,' said Aunt Zofia, venturing out for bread.

Once more a small parcel of butter appeared by the door.

8. CAPTURE

Spring 1944

My tenth birthday in January passed without anyone realising, including me. I knew I was growing because my brown coat was miles too short, although I was still thin enough to wear it.

Zoshienka seemed to blossom with the spring. She slept more often in her own bed these days and, on this morning in April, she was especially vivacious and cheerful because a letter had arrived from Sebastian.

I lay in my bed, watching her put on her make-up, looking like a model in her pale blue suit.

'I want to grow up to be like you,' I said enviously.

'You'll do very well as you are!' she beamed. 'I'm nearly twenty-two!'

'Are you?'

I was amazed. She did not look that old.

'When's your birthday?'

'The end of May,' she replied, blotting her lipstick and pinning a blue felt hat firmly to her head with large hatpin.

I jumped out of bed after her.

'I want to make you something special,' I called after her.

She turned and laughed at me, kissed her mother lightly on the cheek, tucked her bag under her arm and left the apartment.

I went to collect the small skeins of silk and wool that Aunt Zofia had shown me how to unpick from old jumpers. I had decided to embroider a handkerchief into a sachet with 'Z' on the front.

Stefan, too, had left to contact Zbyszek in his apartment behind the church. By nightfall neither of them had returned.

At first Mr and Mrs Grudzinski were not unduly alarmed since partisans often kept overnight vigils. But, after several days without seeing either of them, we all became increasingly worried.

56

Uncle Leon, whom I had never heard shout or even lose his temper, was edgy and irritable, pacing the living room floor continuously, head down, hands behind his back. Mira and I kept out of his way.

Aunt Zofia, eaten with anxiety, made us clean the flat over and over while she washed and scrubbed clothes with what little soap she had left and undertook any household tasks that kept her occupied.

At last, unable to remain inside any longer, she took us round to the friend's flat behind the church to see if there was any news.

Our hearts froze as we saw the SS seal nailed to the door.

'Property belonging to the German Reich'

It confirmed that all who had been in the flat were now in the hands of the Gestapo, known for torturing their victims to death. Everyone's life was in grave danger.

We tore round to the church.

'Father, something has gone terribly wrong,' Aunt Zofia whispered to Father Yuri.

'Go back, work out how you can hide the children. It's likely you'll get a call from the SS,' he advised. 'I'll try to discover what's happened.'

That evening, Aunt Zofia's ashen face peered at him when he knocked on the door. He entered quickly and stood in the centre of the room. He shook his head hopelessly.

'It's not good news,' he said. 'Zoshienka was with Karzymiez, the leader of our resistance group, when the SS stormed the flat. He managed to escape out the window while they looked through his papers, but I am afraid Zoshienka has been arrested. She is detained in the notorious Pawiak Prison.'

Aunt Zofia stifled a scream and wept silently as she realised the hideous experience her daughter was going through.

'People don't come back from there,' she whispered.

'And Stefan?' Uncle Leon's voice was hoarse with emotion.

'The Gestapo found the address book in Karzymiez's jacket. The whole unit has been blown. Everyone has been picked up.'

Uncle Leon started pacing like a caged lion, more and more withdrawn, as he realised he was unable to do anything to secure the liberty of his beloved children.

What horrific fate awaited them could only be imagined, especially if the Grudzinski family were found to be harbouring a Jewish child.

Hourly we waited for the SS to knock on the door to discover me and arrest us all.

We were terrified, but next morning Aunt Zofia said firmly, 'We won't stay here to be captured.'

Without further ado, she decided she would hide us immediately. She knew of a house nearby with a cellar that belonged to the relative of a neighbour across the landing.

She organised us to gather together blankets, candles and an electric ring and we left the apartment, skirting around the back streets and into the house with the cellar.

We were expected and were ushered through a wooden door down steep, stone stairs. Light filtered into the huge space through basement panes. It was cold and eerie. Mira and I held hands tightly as we stood staring at the pile of coal in one corner and the potatoes stacked in another.

'This is a good hiding place for a while,' said Aunt Zofia. 'Come, help me make beds in this corner,' she added.

Sacking had been left in a pile and we set about arranging the blankets as comfortable as possible on top of them.

'You see, you will be quite cosy here and much safer,' said Aunt Zofia, 'but I shall have to return to the apartment every day to see to Uncle Leon.'

Uncle Leon had absolutely refused to leave the apartment in case of any news. She plugged the electric ring into the light socket and we baked potatoes, which we munched in their jackets, while Aunt Zofia left us to go back home.

Although it was dark and creepy down there, we did feel safer now and not at all hungry with hot potatoes inside us. We waited for hours before we heard Aunt Zofia's footsteps again.

'Do we have to stay here forever?' asked Mira.

'No, but until we know for certain . . .'

'I want to stay with you,' whined Mira.

Aunt Zofia sighed deeply.

'Oh, very well. It's safe enough this evening in the house for a while. Come along, both of you.'

We gladly followed her upstairs to the ground floor into a large, ornate room where there was no daylight at all because the curtains were tightly drawn. An oil lamp glowed above a very old man who leaned, as if he was half asleep, over a small, round table covered with green baize.

Our elderly neighbour sat one side of him and the grey-haired lady, whose house it was, the other. They all nodded greetings and Aunt Zofia motioned us to sit on a sofa at the side while she took her place at the table.

I thought they were about to play cards or dominoes, but something very odd was going on.

'What are they playing?' I whispered to Mira.

'It's a séance.'

'What?'

'You get news from the other world,' she whispered.

'Shush!' said Aunt Zofia.

'Are we ready?' began the old man.

He set a paper on the table and placed a plate in the centre of it then he dimmed the lamp above him.

'Hold the plate lightly,' he instructed the women.

They sat absolutely silent and still, hardly breathing, fingers touching around the edge of the plate.

Suddenly it gave a lurch, tipped and slowly began to rise.

I crept up behind Aunt Zofia, my eyes glued to the drifting plate.

'Ask now,' instructed the old man.

'Is Stefan alive?' said Aunt Zofia.

The plate remained suspended.

'Is Stefan alive?' she repeated more strongly.

The plate moved towards 'YES' on the paper.

The old man started to gasp for breath.

'Ask again,' he rasped.

'Is Zoshienka alive?'

The plate hovered and then drifted over 'MAYBE' and then 'NO' and then back to 'MAYBE'.

All of a sudden, despite myself, I blurted out, 'Is Mamushia alive?'

The plate moved with a jerk back to 'NO'.

The spell broke as someone screamed out, *'NO!'* and started yelling.

It was several seconds before I realised it was me. Aunt Zofia was shushing me with her arms about me, rocking and soothing.

'Come, Genia, it may not be right. Look how it hovered over Zoshienka, back, forwards, maybe – nothing is certain.'

She tried to stop my tears, but I felt instinctively that it was so. I wanted to believe her, but I knew my mother was dead.

Much to Mira's annoyance, I cried throughout the night on our bed of sacking.

* * * * *

Three days later Aunt Zofia raced down the steps into the cellar beaming and waving a letter written in German.

'It's from Stefan!' she cried. 'He's all right and he wants us to send him a parcel of food.'

We cheered up immediately. Everything was going to be all right after all.

'I'll take a few potatoes for him, and bread and onions . . . and we have a nice lump of pork fat at home.'

She was fussing with relief.

'Stay safely here,' she warned us. 'I'm going to take the parcel round to Father Yuri. He is allowed into the prison without any problem.'

After that, all was quiet. Uncle Leon reported that no one had called and it seemed the SS were not chasing me after all. We waited in hiding for four weeks until it was decided we could return safely.

It was good to be released from the stuffy cellar into the fresh air. Birds sang in the nearby park and Mira and I skipped behind Aunt Zofia, who hurried ahead.

Along the streets were the rounded advertising posts where Germans pasted bulletins directing people to report for forced labour or listing prisoners who had been shot. Mira and I scanned the lists as we walked home, just in case.

On one orange poster, naming those in alphabetical order who had been shot in Pawiak Prison as 'traitors', we saw:

'Grudzinski, Zoshienka, born 31.5.22. Died 17.5.44'

Mira clasped her hands to her mouth. I wanted to scream out to Aunt Zofia but I realised it wasn't safe to show any reaction.

'I'll tell her when we are inside,' Mira whispered.

We could hear Uncle Leon and Aunt Zofia weeping together in their room that night.

Next morning, Aunt Zofia had pulled herself together and was trying to carry on as if nothing had happened.

Uncle Leon stared silently at the walls and said nothing.

9. DANGER

Summer 1944

Aunt Zofia never talked about Zoshienka, but she worried aloud constantly over Stefan. Food and fuel were extremely scarce and only those with plenty of money survived by paying huge amounts for simple goods like eggs, milk, sugar or butter. Most people had to do without. Aunt Zofia managed to sell her clothes, little by little, to keep us fed, until she was left with only a coat and dress.

The weather was unusually hot. In spite of the constant dusting and mattress beating the apartment was never free of bugs and cockroaches that multiplied in the heat.

'Look, there's one!' we shouted as it scampered behind a cupboard.

We hunted down the bugs and burnt them with candle flames . . . one, two, three . . . dead!

Lice appeared in my hair and made tiny scabs on my scalp that itched madly.

Aunt Zofia despaired of keeping us clean because the water supply was often cut off and she had no more soap. Our hands and faces where wiped with damp towels and our underwear occasionally soaked. It was all that could be done.

Sometimes planes droned overhead. There were many air raids and the sound of guns could be heard in the distance, indicating heavy fighting some miles way. Shells occasionally came whistling into the city followed by loud explosions which sent dust clouds high into the sky, obscuring the sun.

News was scarce, no word from Janina or parcels from the country for months. Uncle Leon went out daily to work the allotment, glean news or see colleagues.

I knew that Aunt Zofia gathered all her strength to keep going for the sake of Mira and me, the little Jewish girl. All of us were slowly starving. Then, at last, brown paper parcels from the country managed to arrive on the doorstep once more.

Father Yuri called to request us to resume the messages.

'We need your help,' he said.

'What harm can two small girls come to?' worried Aunt Zofia, but we pleaded to be able to go.

Thin and wan-looking, we took the tram ride over the bridge to deliver a small portion of butter to the doctor's.

Warsaw was almost under siege with muffled gunfire in the distance. German soldiers nervously patrolled the streets and I saw them rounding up suspects.

We were expected at the surgery. Mira was given money for the butter and then we were pinned with messages.

'You are not to go to the church today,' said the doctor's wife. 'We think the church is being watched. Make sure you don't stop there.'

She drew a little map showing a road not far from Jagellonska.

'You are to go here instead.' She pointed to a square. 'Do you know this building?'

'Yes,' said Mira decidedly.

I suddenly felt uneasy. Up until now our missions had always gone smoothly. The church was a safe haven, but this new address made me feel very nervous.

We sat quietly in our seat during the journey back when the tram suddenly jolted to a halt and we lurched forward.

Soldiers jumped aboard shouting at the passengers to dismount.

'There are Jews on this tram! Everyone get out!' they screamed.

I could not move. Mira grabbed hold of me and pulled me off.

'It's all right. Stand there and don't say a thing,' she hissed.

Rifles pointed over our heads as we stood, small and timid, by the grown-ups.

Everyone protested loudly that they were not Jews and shrugged as they produced identity papers. The soldiers did not think that two children were worth bothering about so we were all let back on to continue the journey over the Kerbedzie Bridge.

One passenger winked at another.

'They're getting edgy,' he remarked.

'Told you it would be all right,' said Mira.

It was about five in the evening when we alighted at the usual bus stop. Mira led me past the church, on past our turning and further down the road right into a broad street lined with elegant houses. We easily found the block of private apartments and nervously entered the main hallway.

We were not at all sure of our reception as we climbed to the third floor and knocked on the door with a special rap. An attractive lady answered the door and, with a smile, showed us inside. She knew exactly where to look for the notes, which she quickly unpinned and handed to a man who appeared from the kitchen.

'You're clever little girls, aren't you?' he said. 'But you will never remember coming to this address – will you?'

At the very moment we shook our heads solemnly in this conspiracy there was a deafening bang. I was engulfed in a haze of horror and then blackness as I was knocked unconscious.

I came to under a pile of bricks and splintered wood, smelling of plaster dust. I could hear people screaming.

Slowly, in the confusion, I distinguished Mira's voice shouting, 'Genia, where are you?'

I tried to say, 'I'm here, help me,' but as I opened my mouth, dust and sand sifted into it and I started to choke. I could hardly breathe, let alone talk.

'Genia! Genia!'

Someone was clawing at the rubble. Suddenly Mira's face, covered in powdered plaster, peered down at me.

'Get up!' she ordered.

I tried lifting myself from the debris. Mira grabbed me with both hands and hauled me out.

All the time she shouted, 'Speak to me! Are you all right? Say something!'

Dry plaster dust and grime clung to my face and inside my mouth suffocating me and I could not say a word.

Somehow Mira managed to stand me on my feet and give me a good shake. That did the trick. It dislodged the obstruction and at last I was able to take a deep breath.

At first I could not remember where I was. My head ached and I felt sick. Mira had her arm under mine and got me to the side of what had been the room. A shell must have exploded on the building, blowing out windows and bringing down floors and walls in a shower of brick, dust and glass.

The ceiling above us was half caved in, leaving splintered, wooden beams rocking precariously. There was a gaping hole in the floor where the edge of the carpet sagged alarmingly. The woman who had let us in was standing in a daze, covered in debris. The man was not there anymore.

My head felt very sore. I could feel warm liquid streaking down the back of my neck. When I carefully touched it and withdrew my hand it was covered with blood.

I screamed, 'I'm dying!'

'No, you're not!' insisted Mira.

'I'm bleeding!' I wailed. 'I'm going to die!'

'Quickly, let's get out of here,' said Mira, sensibly. 'Let's get to Mama before you do.'

She dragged me to the front door which was hanging on its hinge and we managed to slip and slide our way down the stairs which were half-blocked with debris.

Outside, we could see where part of the building had been completely blown away. Several bloodied bodies lay in the street but we did not stop to look.

All the way home I wailed, 'I'm going to die!'

'Stop yelling, you'll live!' Mira bullied me along, half carrying, half dragging me.

She left me sobbing at the bottom of the staircase and went for her mother. Aunt Zofia came running down, gasped when she saw me, gathered me up and rushed me in to the kitchen.

I sobbed, 'It hurts!'

'You must let me find where the wound is,' said Aunt Zofia.

She lifted me over the basin and gently moved my hair apart. Blood trickled into my eyes, down my nose and dripped into the pan. I kept on crying.

'You have a cut. I can see the skull.' She was matter-of-fact. 'Don't worry, it's not so bad. I will bandage it.'

I howled louder.

'Genia, listen to me. I can't take you to a hospital so I am going to clean it myself with iodine. It might hurt a bit.'

As the iodine hit the wound, it burned so much that I screamed and wept even more.

She held me tightly until I began to calm down.

'You're a brave girl,' she crooned. 'Now you don't want to have a big scar on your head, do you?'

I shook my head dumbly.

'I'm going to push it together and bandage you up so you will be as good as new.'

She could not stitch up the wound so she used one of her dolly pegs for a suture. Gradually she pressed the loose skin together and pushed on the peg to seal the gaping injury.

All the time she pleaded, 'Don't cry now, don't cry,' but it was impossible for me not to shriek.

'See, that's done! Look, now we will bandage.'

She and Mira tore up thin strips of sheet then they wet them under the tap and tied them under my chin and up to the top of my head, winding them round and around. It was such a painful operation that I cried continuously.

Aunt Zofia tried to soothe me.

'Cry then – it will hurt less! You know what? You're making me cry too!'

When it was done, she pulled such a funny face that it almost made me laugh.

'Look, I feel your pain too,' she went on, cuddling me and pretending to cry herself. 'It hurts me too!'

'You look just like a corpse!' said Mira.

By now the bandage was pulled so tight under my jaw that I could only make a moaning sound. I was put to bed and tucked in.

'I'll stay and talk to her,' suggested Mira.

'No, leave her alone to sleep,' said her mother, putting a hand tenderly on her shoulder. 'I'll see to you now.'

The bandage slowly dried becoming tighter and tighter. For hours I lay on my side in a swoon, woken by the pain in the night to see Aunt Zofia anxiously hovering over me.

When daylight came, I was gently propped up to take sips of water, but I was so weak I could not even raise my arms to hold the cup.

Some time later, Aunt Zofia turned me on to my stomach and felt under the bandage for the peg, which she lowly pulled out.

'Now it will hurt you less, but it may bleed,' she warned. 'So if you see blood on the pillow, don't make a fuss, it's nothing to be worried about. Try and lie quietly in the dark until you heal.'

She closed the brocade curtains against the light.

'Where's Uncle Leon?' I muttered.

'He'll be back later,' she replied.

I remembered that during one of my bouts of semi-consciousness I sensed his presence, sitting by the bed, talking softly to me.

'Raus! Raus!' Even through the pain, I jumped in terror at the German commands in the courtyard below.

Light flooded into the room as Aunt Zofia opened the curtains and stared down.

'Oh my God!' she cried. 'They're taking Leon!'

She watched from the window as Uncle Leon was forced to join other men on a deportation march. All able-bodied men on the Praga side the River Vistula were being rounded up. There was nothing she could do to prevent it. In the distance, gunshots and explosions peppered the heavy silence.

Aunt Zofia's strength of character and her determination not to give in to the Nazis held her together yet again. She devoted herself to her girls, especially to nursing me better.

The days passed into nights in a fog of fear and pain. I developed a high fever and lay close to death. Always, when I regained consciousness, Aunt Zofia would be nursing me, wetting my lips with cool water, tenderly wiping my face, washing my thin body down with warm water.

Where was Mamushia? Where were Grandfather and Chucha? Where was Tatush? Why didn't they come to see me? Their faces peered down at me in feverish dreams.

Very gradually, I began to recover enough to sip the gruel that Aunt Zofia spooned into my mouth. I lay inert as Aunt Zofia prepared the banki. These were special glasses, heated over a candle flame and placed on my back for a few minutes, warm like a poultice, making red patches on the skin.

Afterwards she rubbed me all over and wrapped warm blankets around me. Large tears trickled down my pale face as the sensation brought back memories of my visits to the bathhouse, but I did not say why I was crying.

Mira's tired face appeared several times at the door, but Aunt Zofia shushed her out.

'Isn't she better yet?' asked Mira impatiently.

'No!' retorted her mother.

But now that Uncle Leon was no longer with us, her mind was made up.

'As soon as she is on her feet again, we are going to get out of Warsaw.'

10. ON THE FARM

October 1944

Now that she had lost two children and her husband, Aunt Zofia was determined to get as far away as possible from the perils of war in Warsaw. She waited until I was strong enough and then told us we were leaving.

'My relative is a railway signalman. He lives at Kotski, just north of here, a little place in the middle of nowhere. We shall be safe there. We'll wait there until the war is over.'

Before the sun was up, with no more luggage than a small holdall, she set out from Jagellonska 32. Mira walked one side of her, I was on the other with bare feet, because I had long outgrown my brown lace-ups.

German reprisals were taking place in the centre of the city, making it far too dangerous to go to the main railway station. We turned and walked towards the outskirts. Once away from the built-up areas, we walked for hours along dusty, country roads.

It was an Indian summer. We stopped now and then to rest on the warm banks, picking ripe blackberries from the hedgerows. Sometimes a cart, loaded with hay or swedes, trundled by and more often than not the driver offered us a ride.

Eventually, we came upon a railway line and followed it along to a small station. No one appeared on the wooden platform, so we sat in silence, listening for the chuff of a steam engine away in the distance.

At long last, a train pulled in, halted and a postman appeared in time to pick up boxes and sacks that were thrown out.

We climbed on board for the journey, stopping and starting along the way. Perhaps I was on my way to Radom. I hoped beyond hope, watching fields and forests hurry buy.

The train drew to a halt at the village of Kotski. Just as we dismounted behind Aunt Zofia, a man in uniform came running

69

along the platform to embrace her warmly. He was Jan, Zofia's cousin, the local signalman. He hurried us into his house nearby.

Hot tea was served by his wife whilst they all exchanged news and discussed the problem of harbouring a Jewish child. They were naturally nervous, especially since many German troops used the railways, so it was decided the best thing to do would be to send me to Jan's brother, who lived on an isolated farm, six miles from the railway station.

The three of us slept together in one bed that night in the signalman's home.

I was dismal next morning as I put on my brown coat and went outside. Jan lifted me on to his cart and then jumped up beside me.

Mira and Aunt Zofia stood on the road, waiting to wave farewell.

'You know we are here. It's not so far, so we shall see each other soon,' Aunt Zofia assured me, seeing my downcast looks.

There was a huge lump in my throat, and my heart sank as the horse responded to the reins and the cart jolted forward. I turned to wave goodbye with tears welling up. I had grown to love Aunt Zofia dearly.

The signalman whistled softly to the horse as it jogged along the dusty racks. The autumn sun cast long shadows of branches overhanging the lanes. I studied the movement of the horse's rump; he had a resolute plod which suddenly reminded me of Srebro and Kasztan, Zygmund's horses, and the outings to Garbatka. Grandfather seemed to be very near.

Finally, we approached an isolated farm where an elderly farmer, shoulders bent from years of labour, stood waiting for the cart to turn in to the yard. The smells and sounds about the place reminded me of the timber yard and my spirits lifted as I jumped down, sending the hens squawking in all directions.

'Well, well, here's a pretty little girl to stay with us,' said the farmer as he led us into the main room of the farmhouse.

He was tall and rugged; once he had been handsome and upright, but now his back was bent from years of hard work. His rotund, little wife appeared, wiping floured hands on her black and grey striped apron. She, too, was wizened and elderly with grey hair pulled back into a bun. She rasped as she breathed, but her warm, blue eyes beamed at me.

'We'll soon put roses back in your cheeks, little one,' she said. 'Are you hungry?'

I nodded shyly.

'Come, eat,' she invited.

She walked heavily, in her lace-up boots, to the scrubbed, wooden table where she cut thick slices of freshly baked bread which she buttered liberally and topped with homemade plum jam.

This must be where all the butter and cheese came from! I suddenly realised the connection between the farm, the signalman and those regular brown paper parcels that had been delivered to the door.

'I think I shall like it here!' I reflected as I took in the whitewashed walls decorated with woven rugs and the picture of Santa Maria over the doorway.

Instead of the terror of war and the terrible conditions in Warsaw, instead of never having animals nearby except cockroaches, I was inundated with the sounds, sights and smells of the farm and I loved it.

The weathered faces of the farmer and his wife looked approvingly as I tucked into the food.

Their daughter, Olga, sat in a rocking chair in the corner, busily knitting, without saying a word of greeting.

'You must call me Babcha (Grandma). I shall enjoy having a child around the place,' said the farmer's wife. 'Olga will never have children!'

She snorted disparagingly at the thought of her middle-aged, spinster daughter. Just like Ma Becky!

'Tomorrow you will meet my son when he comes to work on the farm. He lives in the village with his wife and baby. They cannot help us with all the work – but you can!'

There was no electricity on the farm and that night I went to sleep by candlelight on a woolly sheepskin in a bed-cupboard set into the wall next to the fireplace. The stove had a metal door for wood or coal to be fed into the fire. Here it burned and glowed, night and day, inside the chimneybreast, warming the whole room. In winter, the bed-cupboard would prove to be the snuggest place of all.

The horrible gnawing of hunger in my stomach had disappeared and, at last, I felt quite safe.

I was awakened in the early morning by the sound of a cock crowing and the old farmer stoking up the fire.

'Call me Dziadek,' he smiled. 'Come, we have a job for you.'

As I jumped down, Dziadek (which is Polish for Grandpa) waited for me to slip on my dress then took my hand firmly and led me out into the yard. The air was still damp and misty as he filled the pigs' trough with milk, peelings and leftovers.

Then he let me help him scatter grain on the ground for the hens. As soon as they came clucking for food, he showed me little nooks and corners from where he deftly collected the unattended eggs.

'Will you do this job for me from now on?' he asked, handing me the light, straw basket for carrying eggs.

'Oh yes! Of course!'

He chuckled as he showed me how to put straw in different places to tempt the hens to nest and lay their eggs. I learnt quickly because I was more than eager to help.

It was a small farm with twelve cows, about twenty sheep, a hog and a sow that produced eight or ten piglets a year to sell at market or make into meat. There were ducks and chickens running free.

Work on the farm was never-ending. Dziadek attended to the animals, chopped wood, harvested the land, stored the grain and brought the stores of potatoes, carrots, swedes and onions into the cellar for the winter.

Each morning at dawn, eggs had to be collected. Each day, the cows' milk was separated to make clotted cream, or churned into butter or set for cheese. Each day the animals had to be fed and grazed.

The first morning, Dziadek wanted to show me how to milk a cow, but I was too frightened of the huge, docile creatures to go near.

Still, I was content looking after the hens.

When I brought in my basketful of eggs, Babcha would put some on one side for baking then she showed me how to crack a dozen eggs without losing any yolk and how to scramble a huge omelette for breakfast.

We ate at the large table together with Dziadek's son, Mietek, a sturdy, young man. After breakfast, Babcha sometimes made bread, kneading the dough, leaving it to rise and then forming little loaves or she pickled cabbage or bottled the last of the blackberries and apples. All was preparation for the long, winter months ahead and every morning was filled with farm work and cooking.

I suddenly felt happy in a world so different from hiding, hunger and fear that was part of every day in Warsaw.

Very often, Olga did not appear until mid-morning. She had been a seamstress in Warsaw and hated having to give up her life there for safety's sake. She occupied the one and only bedroom which was out of bounds to everybody else on the farm.

Here she had stacked her possessions including her own pine furniture, the sewing machine and dressmaker's dummy. She spent long hours locked away like a recluse.

Olga was the only person in the family who could read. Occasionally she asked me into her private, neat room to talk about the old days in the city.

'Can I see your books?' I asked. 'Will you read to me?'

I was disappointed when she refused to let me touch them. There were no other books on the farm, not even a Bible.

I began to grow fitter and taller on the wholesome, nourishing food. Nothing fitted me anymore. Babcha searched around to find me a pair of boots and some warm clothes for the winter.

Now the evenings were drawing in and paraffin lamps were lit. Babcha showed me how to use the wooden spinning wheel to turn natural sheep wool into yarn. When there was enough to wind into a large skein, she brought out metal knitting needles and taught me to knit.

At first, I was all fingers and thumbs trying to cope with the metal needles and the wool all at the same time: push through, thread round, pull back, make a stitch.

'Oh dear,' I sighed.

When the day's work was done, Dziadek sat contentedly by the fire rolling his own cigarettes. He waited until Babcha bustled out.

'Don't worry about that.' He winked at me, struggling with the needles. 'Put it away. No more work.'

From his pocket, he produced several stones then he lowered himself onto the sheepskin rug and placed a flat cushion between us.

He chuckled loudly as he taught me how to play 'fivestones'.

'Throw up one, pick up one. Throw up one, pick up two . . .'

'Why are you lazing about? You should be letting her practise knitting,' tutted his wife when she returned.

'And who will keep me company?' replied Dziadek and they both laughed heartily.

The games were fun and somehow Dziadek kept dropping his last stones so I always won.

Eventually, I got the hang of knitting and proudly completed a dozen lines without losing a stitch.

Soon I had knitted enough for a scarf for Dziadek, which Babcha cast off for me.

'Now you can make yourself some winter socks,' said Babcha, casting on again. 'I will turn the heel for you.'

It was greatly satisfying to wear your own, homemade socks, however itchy, and with Babcha's guidance I was soon busy knitting bed socks and slippers for everybody.

* * * * *

The routine of the farm kept everyone busy, but on one Saturday morning, Olga announced over breakfast that she was going into the village and I could go along if I liked.

'Will I see Aunt Zofia and Mira?' I wanted to know with a surge of excitement.

I was eager to tell them all my news.

'I expect so,' nodded Olga, as she firmly pinned on her hat and turned to pick up a parcel of butter and cheese.

The fine weather still held. The tracks were hardened dry. We walked together over farmland, startling rabbits in the grass as we crossed fields of rye, banking down towards a stream which rippled over flat stones.

There was no bridge so we had to ford it, holding our boots high, whilst the cold water swirled around our bare ankles. We continued walking barefoot until they dried.

It was midday by the time we arrived at Jan, the signalman's house and I joyously ran ahead into Aunt Zofia's arms.

'I told you I should be here waiting for you,' said Aunt Zofia. 'Have you been a good girl?'

'Oh yes! It has been such fun.'

I glowed as I grabbed Mira's hand.

The two of us sat close together as I eagerly related my adventures on the farm.

11. WINTER

December 1944

After that visit to the village, I settled even more happily into farm life. Each morning, when the cock crowed, I rose, wrapped up warmly then fetched the grain bowl to go out into the yard to feed the hens. I threw out handfuls of barley and wheat and they pecked around my feet, plump and clucking. I loved their speckled feathers and bright eyes.

Soon I was able to recognise individual birds and some were friendly enough to eat from my hand, especially one large, white, pert fowl.

'You shall be called Tania,' I decided as I searched hidden corners and nooks, filling my egg basket.

By the time the household was awake and busy, I had gathered around two dozen, warm, brown eggs and taken them to Babcha for a delicious breakfast of scrambled egg with pieces of dried meat.

By the middle of December, cold winds swept in from the east, the weather began to worsen and the farm was battened down for the winter.

The yard became a quagmire. It was too sloshy to walk in without putting on galoshes.

Everything became caked with mud and everyone's boots had to be dried off on the stove.

Dziadek brought stacks of wood to the door to make sure we were always warm.

Visiting the village became impossible. Olga shut herself away for long hours and Mietek, the farmer's son, appeared only spasmodically.

One cold, calm day he arrived in the cart with his wife and baby, all wrapped in fur. Babcha cuddled her grandchild delightedly and proudly showed him to me. She called for Olga to come and see, but it was a long time before she opened her door.

The whole family sat down to a meal of chicken stew, bowls of potatoes in cream, mashed carrots and onions. They finished with a special butter cake with hot jam poured over the top.

There was a sense of hope during the meal as I listened to them discussing the progress of the war.

'The Russians are advancing,' said Mietek.

Dziadek shook his head.

'There is no end to this war,' he said. 'Even if the Germans are defeated, our war is still not finished.'

'That's true, the Russians are moving through this area now,' observed Mietek. 'I haven't seen a German for weeks.'

Everyone at the table, especially me, was relieved that Germans had never approached the farm. Nothing threatened me here.

'Where's Tania?' I asked Dziadek next day.

'Who?' he said.

'My little white hen with the speckled chest. She likes me.'

Dziadek roared with laughter.

'If I'd known she was your friend,' he exclaimed, 'we wouldn't have eaten her yesterday for Christmas dinner!'

*　*　*　*　*

January 1945

After Christmas, the weather worsened. Snow blizzards whipped over the land and snowdrifts piled against the walls of the cowshed and barns. Icicles hung from the thatched roof of the farmhouse. The pump handle was frozen solid so Dziadek had to pour hot water on it before he could draw water from the well.

The farm animals were moved into the barn and lived on hay and scraps. Stores were getting lower and most of the hens had stopped laying.

The farm was completely isolated as snowdrifts blocked the tracks and piled against the door. There was no possibility of getting to or from the village and no one knew how the war was progressing . . . until the Russians arrived.

They appeared late one afternoon, at the beginning of January, after a snowstorm, on foot and horseback, dressed in furs and well provisioned. They bivouacked just beyond the farmyard, setting up a field camp. They requisitioned fresh milk and cheese from the farm, vegetables, a sack of barley and a couple of chickens. Their fires glowed as they sat eating camp stew and telling stories, laughing and joking into the night.

'I want to know what's going on in the outside world,' said Olga next morning.

Off she went to the camp, praying that the war was over and her beloved Warsaw liberated.

The news was only fair. There was a big push by the allies but the Germans were counterattacking. Nothing was over and fighting in Poland was intense.

These Russians were hoping to stay a while longer before they moved to the front line.

Olga was consoled by a burly soldier who came every evening for the next couple of weeks and sat with her on a bench by the window. I caught them kissing and cuddling.

Olga's spirits revived. She smiled a lot and sat humming at her sewing machine, making him a warm undercoat. She helped Babcha make cakes which she took to the men encamped nearby.

But their stay was short-lived. When they moved towards the Front, Olga became very morose and lay inert in her room for days, with Babcha fussing over her and Dziadek completely ignoring her.

However, soon there was something much worse to worry about. The next contingent of Russians arrived. An officer, with stars on his uniform, appeared in the yard. He had very little Polish and nobody understood one word of Russian but what he wanted was very plain. He ordered some of his troops to kill the livestock.

Suddenly the pigs and chickens were being slaughtered then the cows were herded out.

'I need this to feed the army,' he said in broken Polish.

He organised men to remove the last sacks of grain and vegetables.

Dziadek went mad. He tried to place himself between the men and his animals. He pleaded with the Russians.

'For God's sake, we are going to starve,' he screamed then he threw himself to the ground on his knees and begged them to leave something, just something, so that we could eat. The officer merely turned his back and walked away.

Dziadek, sobbing, went after him on his knees, in the mud. Babcha cried out that everything was being stolen.

The officer suddenly turned and yelled in Polish, 'You are bastards!'

He strode over and slapped Babcha hard on her face, knocking her to the ground.

After this onslaught, the carcasses and provisions were thrown onto carts and they left.

Dziadek walked heavily over to his wife, put his arm around her and helped her back into the farmhouse.

I attempted to round up the few remaining hens in the yard when I heard a soft lowing coming from the barn. I ran to the barn and then back, bursting into the farmhouse, breathless and excited.

Everything's going to be all right,' I shouted. 'They've left us one cow!'

12. JOURNEY TO WARSAW

March 1945

Throughout January and February, the family managed to live on cabbages and potatoes, with creamy milk and butter from the cow. The farm was still isolated and occasionally, snow fell lightly making the mud tracks smooth and clean.

In early March, new chicks miraculously appeared as fluffy balls of pale yellow, chirping and hopping around their mother hens. Thrilled, I held one in the palm of my hand, feeling its tiny heartbeat.

The old sheep were lambing and the farmer's son brought two piglets up from the village.

'Please take me to visit Aunt Zofia and Mira,' I nagged Olga.

It had been months since I had seen them. The difficult walk to the village might be possible now the land was drying out. Olga was just as tired of being cooped up as I was.

'We could try to get some news from the village, but it will take ages to walk there,' she argued.

On the first really fine Saturday at the end of March she agreed to go. Dziadek was already in the fields when we set off.

'I'll see you tonight,' I said, waving to Babcha.

We made our way across country to the village and the signalman's house. Excitedly, I ran the last yards to knock at the door. It was opened by the signalman's wife who did not recognise me.

'I've come to see my Aunt Zofia,' I said eagerly.

'Zofia Grudzinski? She's not here,' replied the woman. 'She's taken Mira back to Warsaw.'

I stood there in shocked disbelief. Surely they would never have gone without me? I burst into tears.

'Why? Why?' I cried. 'She said she would be here!'

By this time, Olga had caught up and learned that Warsaw had been liberated in January. Aunt Zofia had decided to return by train in the hope of finding Stefan and Uncle Leon alive.

'I want to go back to Warsaw,' I sobbed, not understanding how Aunt Zofia could have forgotten me.

'How can you do that?' enquired Olga crossly. 'I can't possibly take you.'

'I won't come back to the farm,' I said stubbornly.

No matter how they tried to persuade me, I absolutely refused to go anywhere except to Aunt Zofia.

By late afternoon, Olga, exasperated, left me there.

Jan and his wife hardly knew what to do with such an insistent child, but they were kindly people so that night they made me a bed with rugs on the floor, covering me with knitted shawls and my coat.

'It's very dangerous for you to go into Warsaw,' advised Jan. 'There are soldiers everywhere. In any case, there are no passenger trains running.'

I must have looked very downcast.

He shook his head at me then said, 'I'll see what I can do.'

I waited with them for two days. Occasionally, trains shook the little station house as they passed without stopping.

In the middle of the second night, Jan shook me awake.

'There's a freight train going into the city,' he said. 'The driver is willing to take you, but he may not go as far as Warsaw, maybe only to an outside depot.'

'Oh yes!' I cried, jumping up.

'Now look, you can stay here safely with us for a while. There are Germans still skirmishing the countryside. You may get lost when you reach Warsaw. Are you sure you want to risk it?'

'Yes!' I repeated firmly.

No one had much food, but even so, Jan's wife handed me a coloured hanky with bread and a large piece of dried pork tied up inside.

'It's not a lot,' she smiled apologetically, 'but perhaps someone else will help you on the way. Good luck!'

It was quite dark outside as Jan walked me to the steam engine.

'If you want to come,' shouted down the engine driver, 'stand up here, out of my way.'

The signalman lifted me up onto the footplate as steam hissed in the boiler. Heat from the furnace hit my face as I pressed myself against the back of the open cabin. A footplate man threw huge logs of wood into the fire, the driver saluted farewell, the guard mounted at the back and the train moved forward into the night, gradually picking up speed.

It was difficult keeping my balance on the platform. It jolted and swayed, but I did not mind. *Chugga chugga*, over the tracks it sped, taking me nearer to Aunt Zofia by the minute. I lapsed into a daze, half-asleep and pulled myself awake just in time to stop falling out.

As dawn broke, I could see the ground whizzing by just feet below. Smoke and smuts stung my eyes. I stopped looking down because it made me feel dangerously dizzy. I found a metal handle at the back to hang on to, but I was quite frail and it was harder to stand upright than I ever imagined.

After a time, the driver remembered I was there and tied me to the handle with a belt. He and the footplate man seemed to find no difficulty hanging out to look up front or to urinate.

I wanted to too, but when I told the driver all he said was, 'Put your bottom out and do it.'

I didn't dare to, but I was getting desperate. I started crying. They both laughed at me, but the train gradually pulled to a standstill and I was let down to go in the bushes.

'Come on, hurry – I'll go without you!' teased the driver.

On we sped in the dawn light that paled the sky, sending grey mist swirling over the countryside.

Suddenly, with a yell and great swearing, the driver slammed on the brakes and brought the train to a shrieking, skidding halt. If I had not been tied in, I would have slid straight out.

'Well, that's that!' cursed the driver. 'I can't go any further. I've run out of rails. Lucky for me it's light enough to keep a good lookout or we'd have gone straight over.'

We could see that a large section of track had been taken away. Either the Germans or the Russians, or maybe the Poles, had sabotaged it – out in the middle of nowhere.

Everyone jumped down and stood desolately, wondering what to do. There was no sign of civilization, just a wilderness of lonely, misty fields edged with forest.

Several other men jumped off the centre of the train and came along, stamping in the cold, waiting for the guard to join them. Steam hissed in the boiler and then went silent as they stood around considering the problem. There was only one thing to do and that was rebuild the track themselves with the rails from behind.

I climbed back into the cabin and sat, huddled and miserable. There was nothing I could do to help except stay out of the way. Now I would never get to Warsaw or see Aunt Zofia ever again.

Tears streaked my blackened face when I thought of all my plans going wrong. It took hours before some rails from behind were pulled up and re-laid in front. No one had the correct tools to tighten the bolts.

Sweating and swearing, the men strained to secure the sleepers. When they thought it was safe, the driver got the engine up to power and edged the train forward very, very slowly so as not to derail it.

Only a small part of the track could be re-laid at a time. From the back to the front, and again, from the behind to the front. Everyone was exhausted with the effort. It was a nightmare every time the engine moved in case it derailed.

Eventually, they stopped, puffed and weary, to share what food they had with each other, taking the pork I gladly offered them.

'I'll make you something nice when we get going.'

The driver managed a smile.

It took more than two whole days of dismantling and reassembling the rails, the train jolting forward inch by inch, before they managed to join with the old line.

At last, a great cheer went up. The furnace blazed once more, the steam engine turned on full power and the train was able to chug towards Warsaw.

The footplate man held a huge shovel over the heat until it was red hot then he produced a basketful of eggs and some bacon which he fried expertly on the shovel. The aroma suddenly reminded me of Babcha's breakfast and I started to snivel at the thought that I might never see her again – or Dziadek.

The fried eggs and bacon we tipped onto tin plates and shared out. In spite of everything, I was starving hungry and, with the chunk of bread I was handed, I scooped round the plate until it was clean.

'You can stop crying now,' said the driver, cheerfully. 'We shall be in Warsaw by tonight.'

The train arrived at a mainline station on the outskirts of Warsaw that evening. As he pulled to a halt, the driver indicated that I should get out here.

'Do you know where you are going?' he asked.

'Oh yes. And thank you very much for the ride.'

He laughed at my blackened face as he helped me jump off.

I left the station and, like a homing pigeon, made instinctively for the river. I thought I knew where I was, but all the buildings were in ruins and by now it was dark.

I walked for a long time until I came to the River Vistula and headed for the Kerbedzie Bridge, but to my dismay, I could not find it. I panicked, running back along the street straight into a group of soldiers.

I screamed and turned to escape, but my legs collapsed under me and I fell at their feet. After everything, I was going to be shot. I lay face down waiting for the bullet.

It took me a while to realise they were not German soldiers, but Russians.

One of them set me upright and another laughingly said in Polish, 'Are you out to attack us?'

I was not certain of my safety with Russian soldiers either, but I had to tell them why I was looking for the bridge.

'It's not there anymore. It's been destroyed in the fighting.'

'But how am I to get home to Praga district?'

'Follow us!' they said, directing me to a temporary bridge lower downriver.

With a wave, they watched me make my way over that. I could hear the black water running below. Farther away, along the bank, an owl hooted in the darkness.

Within minutes, I found myself on the familiar roads of Praga district. St Floriana's church stood sentinel as I slipped past. An overpowering tiredness enveloped me as I dragged my feet along Jagellonska to the front of the apartments. It was past midnight, but at long last I was safely home.

I reached up by the iron gate and pulled the bell twice. Eventually, an unfamiliar Janitor in his pyjamas and coat, peered out through the patterned gates. To his amazement there I stood, a slip of a girl, filthy dirty from head to foot, demanding to be let in.

'What do you want at this time of night?'

'I want to see Mrs Grudzinski.'

'Come back tomorrow morning.'

'I want to see her now.'

'Go back to where you came from.'

'I came from the station. I can't go back there.'

'I'll not wake her up in the middle of the night for the likes of you.'

This was not getting me anywhere.

'Can I sleep in your flat then?'

'Certainly not. Go away!'

'I can't go away. I live here! I want to be let in now!'

I was determined to be persistent.

'Oh, very well then. I'll take you to Mrs G, but I'm sure she'll throw you out. If she shouts at me, well then you're for it!'

He shook his head, opened the gates and waggled his finger at me.

I followed him through the courtyards, up the three flights of stairs and waited while he knocked on the door then he caught hold of me and held his hand tightly over my mouth.

From inside I heard Aunt Zofia calling, 'Who's there?'

'There's a gypsy girl here. Says you know her.'

I tried to pull his hand away to say I certainly was not a gypsy.

'What's her name?' asked Aunt Zofia's voice.

'I don't know, do I?'

'Ask her!'

The very minute he took his hand away I yelled, 'It's me, Genia, it's Genia!'

The door was flung open.

'Oh, my God!' gasped Aunt Zofia, as she saw the state I was in. 'What's happened? How did you get here?'

What a sight I must have looked. Face blackened and smeared by soot and smoke, my clothes torn, my hair in tangles, my feet bloodied and my thighs red raw from wetting myself.

Aunt Zofia half lifted me into the kitchen where she heated water and bathed me whilst I related the whole story and we wept over each other.

All the goings-on woke Mira who came sleepily into the kitchen and was amazed to find this ragamuffin standing by the sink.

'Look at you!' she scoffed. 'Why did you come back in such a state?'

But Aunt Zofia, cleaning me up with a towel, shushed her by saying softly, 'Where else can she go? She has no other home but this.'

PART TWO

Warsaw to the Holy Land

13. THE JOINT

April 1945

Aunt Zofia's tenderness to me never failed. That night she cuddled both of us in her large, double bed and we all slept soundly. When I awoke next morning I was hungry, ready for breakfast and said as much.

However, unlike the farmhouse, which was barely furnished and full of food, the apartment was full of beautiful objects but the larder was completely empty.

'You should have stayed on the farm,' said Aunt Zofia plainly. 'There you were safe and well fed.'

'But you forgot me,' I complained.

'No, we didn't,' said Mira. 'Mama was coming to fetch you when we had things sorted out. She said so.'

'Well, now you'll be hungry again,' warned Aunt Zofia. 'There's no money left. I shall try to sell something so I can buy food.'

She went into the kitchen to heat water with chicory and we sipped that.

'Now suck a button,' teased Mira.

Once again I felt empty; hunger gnawed and cramped my stomach. No one wanted to buy jewellery or silver or pictures or anything that was not food. Everyone in Warsaw was suffering the same plight.

Aunt Zofia had to eke out whatever she could get to keep us alive. We ate radishes and black bread with occasional white cheese and sucking buttons was the only 'sweet' we had. In any case, there was precious little to buy even if you had the money.

One morning, soon after my return, Izy, the friendly policeman from Radom, stood at the front door with a message from Janina who was safe and well. Perhaps everything was turning back to normal again and I would soon be on the train home to my real family. But there was no news of them in the letter, except to say that certain people were enquiring about the Rapaport family and had contacted her.

Janina wrote they were members of the Polish partisan movement called 'Zob', who had been helping to save Jews. She wanted to know should she tell them about me?

Aunt Zofia read the letter out loud.

'Shall I try to get in touch with them?'

'No!' I said. 'Anyway, who are they? Why are they looking for me?'

'They might want to take you to Jewish people. They may be able to trace your relatives.'

'No!' I insisted. 'I want to stay with you.'

'It won't hurt to let them know about you, at least,' she pointed out. 'Just in case they can help us.'

'All right, then,' I agreed reluctantly.

Mrs Grudzinski gave Izy a note for her sister, agreeing to be contacted by Zob.

'What will they do? Will they write back? Will they come to take me away?'

I constantly worried. Whenever the doorbell rang we all jumped up.

Aunt Zofia ran to the door in hope, saying, 'Maybe it's my Stefan. I hope it's Stefan.'

As for me, I was fearful it was the partisans come to take me away.

At the end of April, there was a knock on the door and this time Aunt Zofia opened it to a small, plain woman, dressed in a dark, shabby suit that seemed much too large for her. Standing behind her were two, skinny, young men.

The woman simply said, 'I know you have a Jewish girl in your flat.'

She spoke in Polish but she had a strong accent.

'Are you from my sister Janina?' queried Aunt Zofia.

'Yes. We are looking for Jews,' she nodded.

Her eyes were bright and her voice sounded young, but she looked old and worn out.

'Come in.'

Aunt Zofia brought the woman and her companions into the sitting room where Mira and I sat apprehensively.

The minute I realised who they were, I started to shake with fright, but the woman smiled at me and spoke quietly as she sat down.

'My name is Paula,' she said. 'I am with the Polish underground organisation called Zob. We work with The Joint.'

'The Joint?' questioned Aunt Zofia.

'It is an American Jewish organisation, set up to help Jews everywhere.' She turned to me. 'Especially to rescue little children like you, to give you a new future in Palestine where you can grow up without fear.'

I eyed her suspiciously.

'We can take you if you want to go,' volunteered one of the men.

'I don't have to go, do I?'

I had absolutely no intention of leaving Aunt Zofia again.

'No. I'm here to help you, whether you want to go along or not,' Paula replied. 'But we will keep in touch with you from now on to make sure you are all right.'

As they rose to go out, the other young man handed Aunt Zofia a brown packet.

'This is dried egg,' he said. 'It makes very good omelettes.'

That afternoon, Aunt Zofia mixed half a cup of the yellow powder with a little water and stirred it in a saucepan over a low heat. Lo and behold, it turned into scrambled egg and we tucked in hungrily.

'You see, I'm glad we got in touch with them,' said Aunt Zofia. 'Next time they come we'll ask them to try to trace your relatives. It won't hurt. Just in case they are worried about you.'

Two weeks passed without anybody from Zob or the Joint calling. The powdered egg had run out and we were starving again.

'Perhaps they are busy,' suggested Mira.

'Perhaps they have forgotten about me,' I said hopefully.

Then one morning, as Aunt Zofia ran to the door as usually, saying, 'Let's hope it's Stefan!' she found a small, wizened, old man standing there.

'I want to speak to the Jewish child. Is she still here?' he asked.

Aunt Zofia half closed the door on him, quickly turned and pushed me into the kitchen.

'Who are you?' she demanded.

'You spoke to the Joint about this child. I'm the translator. They're Americans. I speak Polish. I want to ask her if she wants to come with me.'

'No!' I screamed from the kitchen.

'I haven't come to take her, just her details. Who she is, where she comes from. You know.'

'You can come out, Genia,' said Aunt Zofia. 'No one is going to take you away. I won't give you to anybody.'

She motioned him to sit at the table next to her with me opposite them then he asked question after question.

'What is your real name? Who is your father? Who is your mother? Where did you live? How old are you?'

I found questions about my past upsetting and painful. I tried to recall as much as I could as he jotted everything down on a piece of paper. Aunt Zofia prompted me with answers she knew.

'Might you know anything about her family?' she enquired. 'Are they alive and well?'

He raised his eyes to the ceiling and shrugged then he left saying the Joint would be in touch . . . and they were. The following morning a food parcel arrived with tinned cheese, coffee and sugar. Aunt Zofia was delighted.

'You see, the Jewish people are caring for us.'

Every single day after that someone, either a man or a woman, appeared at the door to hand over a parcel with the words, 'Regards to Genia from the Joint.'

It was better than Christmas and all the good times in one. We eagerly opened the parcels to discover all manner of goods: sugar, tins of fruit, soap, stockings, flour and chocolate.

'Isn't it wonderful to taste chocolate after sucking buttons?' said Mira gleefully.

I certainly agreed.

The next official visit was from Paula who brought along a very fit-looking, well-dressed man.

He said he wanted to speak to Aunt Zofia alone, but she insisted I be there. He spoke Polish fluently, but he evidently had not suffered any hardships. Perhaps he had lived in America?

'I'm here to tell you that we have found other boys and girls who have been in hiding like Genia. We are taking them to Palestine and we want Genia to come too.'

'What makes you think I'll let her go?' said Aunt Zofia. 'How do I know she will be safe? Who's going to look after her?'

He stood up.

'Do you want money for her?'

'How dare you!'

Aunt Zofia was mad at his suggestion. I had never seen her so angry.

'Get out!' she shouted.

Paula put a restraining hand on his arm. He turned and gave a slight bow to her.

'Dear madam, I apologise profusely, but we have had to buy back some of these children. I can see that is not the case with you.'

Aunt Zofia had her arms around me.

'She is like a daughter to me,' she said protectively.

She looked at Paula.

'But I am worried that she needs to find her own family – her own people. Things are so difficult in Poland. We can hardly feed ourselves.'

She shook her head.

'I don't know what to do.'

'Come to my office next week when you have had time to talk it over with her,' he said.

'And don't worry about food. We'll see to it you get enough to manage,' promised Paula.

They went away, leaving Aunt Zofia in a dilemma, talking it over again and again with me and Mira.

'You don't have to go, Genia,' said Aunt Zofia gently. 'On the contrary, I would love to have you stay. If only Uncle Leon were here and Stefan.'

She wiped her eyes on her apron.

'Don't you want to see your family again?' asked Mira.

'Of course I do,' I said, recalling the old times.

'Well then, they may already be in Palestine,' suggested Mira encouragingly.

'You will certainly be among your own people there, Jewish people,' pointed out Aunt Zofia.

She felt that after the tragedy of the Holocaust there was no future for Jews in Poland.

'But I like it here. I want to stay with you.'

'Of course you do. I want you to. Now, while you're young, it doesn't matter, but in the future, when you're grown up, you will want to be Jewish again, especially if you have a family of your own. You see, people belong to each other, they're born into a religion that is theirs. You don't choose it, you just belong to it with your family and that's how you'll want your children to be. I don't ever want you to feel sorry you didn't go.' She paused. 'You can always come back if you don't like it.'

'I don't know what to do.'

I was more confused than ever.

'Tomorrow I'll take you to see the man at the Joint. You can talk to him.'

'All right.'

Perhaps he could sort this out for me.

'Any decision will be up to you alone,' said Aunt Zofia.

'I would go if I were you,' said Mira.

What a good idea!

'Well, come with me,' I said eagerly.

'I have to stay to look after Mama,' replied Mira.

'Let's all go then!' I exclaimed, brightening up at the thought.

'And who would there be to welcome Papa and Stefan when they return?' answered Aunt Zofia.

'It's all so complicated,' I sighed.

*   *   *   *   *

May 1945

We walked to the apartment block where the Joint Jewish Distribution Committee (JJDC) had its offices. The main headquarters were in New York, but contacts had been set up all around Europe; in Switzerland, France, Hungary and Poland. The Warsaw office was in the Praga district since the buildings on the other side of the River Vistula had mostly been destroyed by the retreating Germans.

We were expected. Paula greeted us and showed the three of us into a room where the Polish-American who had visited our apartment rose from his desk. He held a chair for Aunt Zofia, who pulled me onto her lap as she sat down, while Mira stood leaning up against her.

'Well now,' he said directly to me from behind his desk. 'You have come to tell me you want to go to Palestine.'

But I hid my head against Aunt Zofia saying nothing.

She whispered gently, 'No, you must tell this gentleman if you want to go or you don't want to go.'

'If I go, when will it be?'

'Any time you like,' he said.

'I'll think about it and I'll tell Aunt Zofia.'

'That's fine. I'll call next Wednesday and you can tell me yes or no.'

'By next week?'

'Yes, I'll come and you will tell me.'

On the way home, it seemed to be decided.

'You can say yes then if you don't want to go you can change your mind,' said Mira sensibly.

'Even if you go and don't like it you can always come back,' encouraged Aunt Zofia.

'Will you be here for me?'

I wanted to be sure.

'Of course. This will always be your home,' said Aunt Zofia.

I knew this was true. Aunt Zofia never lied.

As promised, the following Wednesday, Paula called, bearing a food parcel. Beside her stood the man wanting my answer.

'All right, but if I don't like it I'll come straight back,' I told him.

'Of course,' he said. 'We will collect you on Friday morning.'

Over the next couple of days, Aunt Zofia tried to talk herself into letting me go.

'If I could give you a safe future, I should never let you leave,' she told me. 'If you want to change your mind at any time you can, you know that.'

I mooched around unhappily.

'You'll be happy there, I know. Perhaps you will find your family. Palestine is a lovely, sunny country. You know you can pick oranges from the trees!'

I sniffed as a tear trickled down my cheek.

'And we'll write to each other and you'll tell me how you are getting on.'

'I'll write to you always,' said Mira.

* * * * *

I could not believe it was our last night together. We slept three in the bed, hugging each other. Over the years that I had

97

lived with them, I had come to love Mira and Aunt Zofia more than I could have imagined. The thought of leaving them made me very miserable.

When morning came, the two young men arrived who had first come with Paula.

'We're here to fetch little Genia,' they said.

'I don't want to go,' I sobbed, but in my heart I knew I had no choice.

My small, hessian satchel was ready, packed with two pairs of knickers, thick socks, a green sweater that had belonged to Mira and a jam sandwich. My old, brown coat, which was miles too short, still fitted my thin frame. In its pockets, I clutched several photographs. One of the Grudzinski family together, one of Mira in the church, one of Zoshienka looking smart and one of Aunt Zofia standing alone.

'These are my only treasures,' I thought.

I threw myself at Aunt Zofia in a final hug. I kissed and hugged Mira, both of us with tears in our eyes then we three followed the men downstairs and through the courtyards.

As soon as we reached the front iron gates, one of the men firmly took hold of my hand and walked me out along the street before I could say another word.

I pulled to look back and saw Mira and Aunt Zofia still waving goodbye. We turned the corner and then they were gone.

14. THE GROUP

'Where are we going?' I asked the men who were quickly walking me away from Jagellonska.

'We're taking you to meet some new friends,' said the taller one. 'I'm one, my name is Yuli.'

He was not old, in his early twenties maybe and sounded Polish. He looked swarthy and Jewish. I wondered where he had hidden during the war. His companion spoke to me as well, but I could not understand his language.

We caught a tram to the riverside, but since the old Kerbedzie Bridge had been completely destroyed, we could only cross the Vistula on foot by the temporary, military bridge that I had used in the dark. We had to catch another tram across the city.

This time I could see for myself the extent of war damage. The centre of Warsaw was gutted. Skeleton buildings stood roofless, their ragged edges pointing to the sky. Many areas were total rubble. Here and there, people picked over the debris searching for belongings. Workmen were clearing sites to make the streets passable. There were tanks and soldiers everywhere in the wider roads, but this time they were Russians.

When we dismounted, I began to I feel just as sick and apprehensive as on my first trip to Warsaw. It seemed so many years ago after all that had happened.

We reached a block of flats, scarred by bullets and entered the hallway. The front rooms of the ground floor apartments had been turned into offices. I held back nervously. Yuli took my hand. Paula appeared to greet me and they led me through the office rooms and opened the door to a back bedroom.

'This is where the children are,' said Paula.

'Come and meet your new friends,' encouraged Yuli.

Several sickly and scared-looking children turned and eyed me. No one said anything. I stood at the doorway clutching my hessian satchel, wishing I had not left Aunt Zofia. Three girls were sitting on a mattress in one corner, several boys squatted on the floorboards the other side of the room.

Eventually, a youth stood up from the group and came over.

'You're the last one. They said there were nine of us – so you're it.'

'Oh.'

I looked up at him. He was extremely tall and thin and seemed to be the oldest.

'I'm Micky,' he volunteered.

He was fair-haired and very good-looking!

'I'm Genia,' I smiled.

'I'm Julie,' said a pale-faced girl, lying on the mattress in the corner.

Her deep brown eyes were ringed with dark shadows of suffering. Her hair was cropped short and she looked painfully thin.

'I'm fourteen,' she added.

'Hello,' I said.

'I'm Shona,' joined in another girl who looked much plumper and healthier than the others. 'I'm thirteen and this is Rene. Come and sit with us.'

Suddenly I did not feel so alone.

'What are they going to do with us?' I asked, sinking onto their mattress.

'They're taking us to Palestine. We don't know when exactly,' said Julie, 'but now you're here I think we will go soon. How old are you?'

'Eleven,' I replied.

'Then you're the youngest. I'm already twelve,' said Rene with an elegant Polish accent.

She sounded very refined. Her clothes were in good condition and her long, fair plaits were bound with ribbons.

'The boys aren't very nice, so we've decided not to have anything to do with them.'

Just then Yuli and Paula reappeared with plates of bread and cheese and mugs of milk.

'Tuck in,' said Yuli cheerfully.

We were all very subdued. No one talked as they ate.

A tall, dark-haired, clean-shaven man of about thirty wandered into the room watching us eat. He observed us with an air of authority.

'That's right, build up your strength,' he advised. 'We've got a long way to go. My name's Katz. I'm your leader. You've met Yuli and Paula. They'll be coming along too.'

Yuli clicked his tongue and winked at us behind Katz's back. We stared at Katz unflinchingly.

'Tomorrow I'll give you instructions,' Katz added.

He turned at the door with a stern look on his face.

'You'd better obey them. Understand?'

We children nodded miserably.

'Here you are, kids,' said Yuli, unwrapping a brown paper packet. 'American chocolate!'

During the day, I exchanged stories with the other girls. Julie's pale, gaunt face was framed by dark, cropped hair.

'I was hidden in a Convent,' she said. 'The sisters were very kind to me, but I had to stay in a cell most of the time because I was too small to be a novice. The Nazis would have realised. The nuns said they prayed for me; they said they were praying for the whole world.'

She looked down at her skinny hands and added, 'There was so little to eat, I was always hungry.

'So was I!' I said.

'I had lots to eat,' confided Shona. Her wide face glowed like a healthy peasant. 'I was on a farm.'

'So was I!' I said. 'For a while anyway.'

'I lived with an elderly, aristocratic lady,' Rene told us.

Her long, blonde hair and blue eyes made her look like any other Polish girl, as I did.

'Because I couldn't go to school the old lady taught me to read from her library of books and I can play the piano!'

'So can I!' I was about to say and then thought better of it.

The boys kept to the other side of the room. They didn't want to mix with girls either.

That night we all lay down on the floor in the clothes we wore. I shared the mattress with the girls, but it was very hard to settle. I had never slept in a room with so many others before.

Several boys coughed incessantly and Julie moaned in her sleep.

When the new day dawned, I felt less like leaving Warsaw than ever. The next couple of days were spent in equipping us with suitable clothes and warning us about the dangers of the journey ahead.

'Here, in Poland, it is still unsafe to be Jewish,' said Katz.

'When are we going?' I interrupted.

'So we are going to pretend to be Greeks,' he continued.

'Why have we got to do that? Are we going to Greece?' I interrupted again.

'No, we're going to get you to Palestine. In the meantime there are gangs round here waiting, wanting to attack Jews.'

'But the war's nearly over,' I said.

'Do you want to be killed?' asked Katz, exasperated.

'No, but . . .'

'No buts,' ordered Katz. 'You talk too much. Yuli, wrap her up!'

Yuli took out a large handkerchief from his pocket.

'If I tie my hanky like this,' he said, putting it under my chin and tying it on top of my head, 'you could pretend to have a toothache.'

All the group laughed.

'Don't do that!'

I ripped the hanky off.

'Tomorrow you'll be wrapped up with a scarf,' said Katz, 'whether you like it or not. We leave tomorrow.'

That night I lay awake, thinking my own thoughts, when Rene whispered aloud, 'Do you think we will see our parents when we get there?'

'I don't want to talk about it,' said Julie.

'Go to sleep,' Shona shushed.

'I want Aunt Zofia,' I thought and buried my head in the mattress to hide my despair.

15. JOURNEY TO PRAGUE

We were given a final briefing by Katz in the morning. Everyone was sworn not to utter a word. None of us wanted to talk anyway. Everyone had suffered in silence for years, keeping their hurt, their fears and all their feelings deep inside. Now we were in shells of our own, afraid of the past, fearful and uncertain of the future.

'Now, remember, you lot! You don't understand Polish,' he said. 'Even if you do understand what is said to you, pretend you don't. And stay close together. No one is to drift off. All you boys are to stay with us no matter what. Micky, you're the oldest so keep your eyes on the group.'

He pursed his lips as he looked at his emaciated charges.

'If we have to split or move quickly, then, Yuli, you stay with the girls.'

'You're a chatterbox.' He pointed at me. 'I can't trust you not to speak. Yuli, tie her up.'

He handed Yuli a roll of bandage and some cotton wool.

'I bet you're good at acting,' suggested Yuli, as he tied the bandage around my head. 'Pretend you have a terrible toothache and just go *arrgghh!* if anyone tries to get you to speak.'

All I could do was nod. We gathered our small bundles of personal things together and set off for the station with Katz at the front and Micky, Paula and Yuli at the back with the girls.

There were plenty of Russian soldiers milling round the streets. They were also on guard at the war-damaged station.

After Katz paid for tickets, he turned to find a soldier barring his way, shouting something in Russian. We stood in a terrified group. They were going to capture us even before we started out.

Katz looked puzzled. He shrugged his shoulders then he said something in another language that I could not understand. He repeated the same word over and over. It must have got home because the soldier nodded and waved us towards the waiting steam train.

Katz did a little 'thumbs-up' as we climbed into a large carriage full of passengers. We had to disperse ourselves around the available seats without talking, just by pointing and indicating. We did not dare to speak Polish.

I sat next to Shona, waiting for the train to move.

'It's taking me away from Aunt Zofia,' I thought miserably as the train rattled into motion.

From deep down came memories of Janina taking me away from Radom. I recalled Grandfather's timber yard, Chucha and Mamushia taking me to the baths, Sabbath candles glowing in the dark, Aunt Zofia's comforting arms. I was leaving the ones I loved again. I could hardly bear it as tears spilled over and slid down the side of my nose.

'Is your toothache hurting you?' whispered Shona in my ear, giving me a little dig.

The journey from Warsaw lasted several hours, stopping and starting along the way. It was late afternoon before we followed each other to disembark at Lublin. We hung around while Yuli went off to find food and came back with three loaves of black bread and pieces of sausage which we shared and ate on the platform. By this time, Katz had found out about the trains.

'There is nothing else going today,' he told us. 'We'll have to find somewhere to spend the night. Stick together.'

We followed the leaders despondently around the town. Poland was full of refugees and no one was willing to help us. By now, we were tired and listless. What were we going to do?

All at once, a group of young thugs appeared, laughing and shouting. They stopped and stared at our group standing on the other side of the street. Then I heard the sickening words as they started to taunt and jeer at us.

'Juden, Juden, are you Jews? Are there still some of you left?'

Katz hissed, 'Move!'

I almost fainted with fear, but I was carried along by the group pretending we did not understand. It proved beyond doubt that Aunt Zofia was right – we were never going to be safe.

We plodded around for ages until eventually Katz said, 'There's nowhere to stay tonight. I'm sorry, but we'll have to sleep in the shop doorways.'

I did not care where I slept. I sank down to the pavement exhausted. The chill of the night seeped through my coat as I huddled with Shona against a shop door. I drifted into a doze, waking several times to see Yuli or Katz walking up and down in front of us on guard.

At dawn, we children gathered, stiff and forlorn, to face another journey to we knew not where. When we returned to the station, we used the toilet to clean up, by which time an early train had pulled in.

This time we claimed two small compartments to ourselves and slept soundly as the train lurched and rumbled along the lines further south towards Lvov.

'We can take this off for a bit,' said Yuli, waking me up by unbandaging my face and handing out portions of chocolate.

I watched the flat fields and forests of Poland hurry past the window. Here and there a small farm holding appeared for a moment and I suddenly recalled Dziadek, with his large, capable hands, reaping the land and milking the cows; and Babcha churning the butter and shaping it into pats.

'I don't suppose I shall ever see them again,' I thought sadly. 'Nor Mira or Aunt Zofia or anybody.'

Once again, the tears welled up and spilled out.

After a run of several hours, the train halted with a jolt. We could hear the guard shouting. Katz slammed the carriage door behind him as he jumped down and walked along the line to find out what was happening. He was soon back.

'It's not going on. The lines are disrupted further down. It's going back to Warsaw tomorrow.'

Dispirited passengers had their heads out of windows, arguing and grumbling. Some were disembarking, making their way back along the tracks to Lublin.

'It's dangerous to hang around. In an hour or two it will be getting dark,' said Katz. 'Get out, all of you, we're not going to spend the night in the cold. Follow me.'

We slid down the embankment and trudged after him across the fields towards the nearest farmhouse.

'Wait here,' he said at the boundary and disappeared behind the outhouses.

'Food and warmth!' he shouted five minutes later.

He had quickly negotiated with the farmer for a sum of money and that night we were billeted in a haystack eating black bread and hardboiled eggs.

None of us said much at first. It wasn't at all what I had been expecting.

'It is certainly an adventure,' thought Rene aloud. 'Living rough.'

It must have been, after her aristocratic existence.

'I don't like it,' I said. 'I want to go back.'

'I don't,' declared Julie. 'Not to the convent anyway.'

'It's going to get worse before it gets better,' warned Shona, tucking into an egg.

The haystack was surprisingly comfortable and warm and, despite the odd accommodation, everyone slept soundly.

When the cock crowed, I thought for one moment I was back on Dziadek's farm. There was a pump in the yard for water to drink and clean up and we went behind the hedge for toilet.

We trudged back to the road and walked for several miles until a farmer with a horse and empty cart offered us a lift to the next town. All twelve of us gladly squeezed into the back and listened to the horse's plod. For a little while, I felt secure.

But we were still in Poland. As we dropped off the back of the cart to walk to the station, another crowd of yobs spat and jeered at us.

'Get out of our town, you Jews, or we'll get rid of you ourselves,' they threatened.

Julie and I grabbed each other's hands, ready to start running the minute they came towards us. Katz looked as if he did not know what they were talking about (although he knew perfectly well) while we huddled closer. There was safety in numbers.

There were plenty of troop trains. Once again, Katz went into negotiation with a truck driver who agreed, on exchange of money, to take us on to Lvov.

We travelled all day, sitting in the back of the truck, swaying and jolting against the boards, with nothing to eat or drink all that time.

At last, weary and tired, we arrived in Lvov and were dropped off at a particular house. We were evidently expected because a welcome hot meal of potatoes and soup was dished out without any more ado. Then we were bedded down on a mattress spread out in several rooms. It was luxury!

That night two more boys were brought in to join the group, together with a couple of young men in their early twenties, one of whom I noticed had a knife tucked into his boot.

'He's going to murder us all in our sleep,' I muttered, frightened.

'No, he's not. He's going to protect us. Go to sleep,' whispered Julie on the mattress beside me.

By now, the weather was wet and windy and Katz felt we should not travel for a while. We were very relieved. We needed time to regain our energy. It was a short stop, only a couple of days and once again we set off by train which was to take us into Czechoslovakia.

The train halted at the border. Soldiers came through the carriages looking at papers. Katz (using a broken Polish accent) explained to the frontier guard that we were Greeks, trying to get home from work camps. Since the whole of Europe was in turmoil, nearing the end of the war, this was not unusual. The guard nodded and asked no more questions.

We finally disembarked at Prague station. Around the area there seemed less war damage. People were going about their business, there were no groups of thugs roaming the streets, no one pointed or jeered at us and the whole atmosphere seemed less threatening.

We made our way to a boarding house which was another rendezvous of the Joint. Here, a kindly landlady gave us a hot meal of thick soup, but it did not cheer me up.

'Are we nearly there?' I wondered wearily.

Several adults were waiting in the Prague house to join our group and there was also one boy. He had a huge, swollen belly, so large he had to support it with his hands underneath whenever he walked. All the boys in the group ignored him.

'What's the matter with him?' I asked Paula.

'His belly is blown out from starvation,' Paula replied. 'His name's Josh. Go and talk to him.'

I went over and said, 'Hello.'

'Hello,' replied Josh.

'Do you hurt?' I was curious.

'Yes, a bit,' said Josh, 'but they're going to make me better in Palestine.'

'It seems a long way away,' I sighed.

'I can't wait to get there,' said Josh.

Just getting out of Poland had taken over two weeks. We were in such low spirits, drained and enervated, no one said much except Katz, who took the initiative.

'Do this, do that.'

We followed instructions like sheep.

Most of the children's energy had been sapped by past experiences and none of them was particularly friendly. It was enough to share a piece of bread together.

I became more depressed at the thought of once more losing my family. The longer the journey took, the lower my spirits became. I just wanted to turn round and go back.

When I slept in all my clothes at night, I yearned for Aunt Zofia's arms to hold me. There was no one to turn to here.

In Prague, we were given days to recover our energy. We went out on sorties with an adult. Prague itself seemed to be recovering from the turmoil of wartime. People in the streets smiled at each other, exchanging greetings. Children with their parents skipped happily along in family groups. It hurt. It made me feel jealous. They ignored the grey faces of us worn out, underfed children.

'They all belong here,' I thought miserably. 'I don't belong anywhere.'

Josh's sunken eyes studied me that afternoon when I returned from a walk.

'I know what you're thinking,' he said, 'but we can't go back.'

'Why not?'

He shook his head.

'It's not the right place for us.'

He spoke with a pure Polish accent. He had obviously come from a good family.

'It was for me,' I said.

'It wasn't for me,' he went on. 'Do you know where I lived?'

I shook my head.

'If I tell you, you won't tell anyone, will you?'

I shook my head again. He came over, holding his stomach with his hand and sat very close to me.

'I don't want them to laugh at me again,' he whispered. 'Promise?'

'I promise.'

'With the pigs.'

'On a farm?'

'In a farm, with the pigs.'

I was horrified as I began to realise what he was saying.

'You mean actually in a pig sty?'

He nodded.

'I had to sleep with the pigs and . . .' he looked away, staring down at his enlarged belly, 'and eat pigswill.'

I opened and closed my mouth without saying a word. I did not know what to say.

'I've got something special in my pocket,' Josh confided. 'It's very important. Do you want to have a look?'

He pulled out a pocket book with a hard, blue cover and carefully, almost reverently, opened it.

Neatly displayed on each page were sets of colourful, unused stamps. Postage stamps.

'Look at them,' he breathed. 'They are Nazi stamps.'

'Oh.'

I had never seen anything like them before.

'I don't show these to just anyone,' said Josh. 'They're special. To remember the past. Never to forget what happened to me.'

'Oh.' I repeated, only half understanding.

'Can I see?' asked Julie, walking over.

'No, they're private,' replied Josh, quickly pushing the book into his jacket pocket.

During the night, sleeping as a group together in a large bedroom without beds, only blankets on the floor, Josh moaned continuously. He was in constant pain and next morning he did not want to touch the breakfast of bread and cheese.

Yuli went out later in the day and brought back some white medicine. He encouraged Josh to take it.

'There are good doctors in Palestine who will make you better,' Yuli promised.

'I just want to get there,' repeated Josh.

16. PRAGUE TO ALBA JULIA

Church bells pealed out as we left for the Prague station.

'The bells are ringing because we're leaving,' Shona said to me, her round face looking wan.

'Nobody wants us,' I agreed.

'Get yourselves into small groups,' ordered Katz. 'It's Easter Sunday and we don't want to look conspicuous.'

The group split into fours and sixes with the leaders arranging to meet up at prearranged points. We four girls and Josh kept together with Yuli. We were in for a hard time, changing trains with short journeys and long stops, gradually making our way into Hungary.

Ours was a sad, subdued little group. Cold, often hungry, dishevelled and dirty. Sometimes we slept in boarding houses, sometimes in station waiting rooms, sometimes in shop doorways, sometimes in haystacks, never in beds.

We lived mainly on bread. Sometimes Yuli got raw carrots or potatoes to add to the diet. Occasionally, he produced a chocolate block from his haversack.

'We're getting there,' he encouraged.

We met up with the others early one evening in Hungary, in a town called Tokay. The scenery about us was beautiful. The whole area seemed covered with lush, forest greenery, dotted with white houses that stood in well-cultivated grounds.

Katz looked at his ragged charges in despair.

'Cheer up!' he said. 'I know of some Jewish people here. They'll look after us.'

'Clean water!' said Julie, looking taller and thinner, her dark hair growing into matted lumps.

'Hot soup,' added Shona, looking less well fed than before. 'With lentils and rice.'

'Clean beds,' breathed Rene, whose hair ribbons hung limp and dirty. 'White sheets!'

'Clean clothes!'

I yearned to get out of the filthy rags I wore.

We followed Katz along the road leading out of town to a large, detached house. We tramped wearily behind him up the long drive edged by grassy banks peppered with daffodils. We could see candles glowing through the windows. At last we felt almost at home.

Katz knocked loudly. A woman answered, wiping her mouth with a napkin. We could hear sounds of merriment from inside and our spirits lifted.

'Yes?'

'We are a group of Jews come from Poland,' he said.

'Oh yes?'

She was indifferent.

'We were hoping to stay with you perhaps?'

She pulled a face and shook her head.

'No. That's not possible. It's all clean for Passover,' she said crossly. 'We can't possibly have such dirty urchins here,' and she rudely closed the door in our faces.

We could not believe it. Katz turned to us, hitting his head with his hands in despair. What unbelievable treatment!

'They didn't even offer us a drink of water, those . . . people!'

He swore loudly before he took us back to the road, hungry, tired, dispirited and by now it was turning dark. Too late to return to the centre of the town.

The leaders went off, looking for somewhere to sleep for the night and came upon a cow byre. We huddled together, tormented by nightmares, trying to keep warm.

It rained during the night. I woke, damp and stiff. My head ached and it hurt when I coughed.

The fields had become a quagmire. In the dark, grey dawn, the group began to make its way back to the road, but I could only drag myself along. The headache was so blinding I could hardly see the others then my shoe stuck in a mud puddle and when I yanked my foot it came out without the shoe which sank still further. No one turned to help me. It was no use, I would have to leave without it.

113

When I caught up with the others, some of the boys laughed at me because I had wiped my tears away with muddy hands.

'Look at her, little one-shoe!'

'Come on,' shouted Katz. 'Keep moving!'

Josh lolloped beside me for a while. He was puffing and blowing, holding up his belly when he walked.

Katz found a little farmhouse and spoke to the farmer who allowed us to sit in the barn. Soon, the farmer's wife brought out bread and warm milk, straight from the cow. None of us said anything, we just passed the mugs around and then lay back with closed eyes, completely worn out.

Josh sat alone, leaning against a hayrick, rocking his body backwards and forwards as if to ease his pain. I crawled over to him.

'Never mind about your shoe.'

He managed a smile.

'Aren't you hungry?'

He had eaten only half his bread.

'Yes, but I am sucking the bread. That makes it last much longer.'

'I used to suck buttons,' I said, wishing beyond reason that I could go back to Aunt Zofia.

The farmer's wife must have noticed my bare foot and the state I was in because, just as we were about to leave the farmyard, she came running out of the house waving a pair of old shoes which she handed to me. They were much too large for my waif-like feet, but since they were all I had to wear I grudgingly put them on.

'Now I really look like a beggar,' I thought ungratefully.

We trudged like zombies back into Tokay. It was drizzling as we made for the shelter of the station, still early in the morning. The train to take us across the border to Rumania was not due until much later, so I used the toilet to try and clean up a little. I wasn't very successful. I had been wearing the same clothes for weeks on end and felt very itchy and dirty.

Once on the train I fell into a fitful sleep, sometimes feeling cold and shivery or hot and aching. I was deeply asleep when we crossed the border and woke feeling better.

This was Oradea that we arrived at in the afternoon.

Katz said, 'We've got a bit of a way to walk. We're going up into the Carpathian mountains.'

Once more, he seemed to know the contact places.

We climbed a winding road strewn with fallen rocks and boulders, slowly making our way up the mountainside until the high walls of a convent rose above us.

Mysteriously, without any sign of a human hand, the large, wooden doors opened quietly the moment Katz was about to knock – as if we had been long awaited.

Not a soul appeared as we walked wearily through the courtyard and around the well in the centre. We stared up at the windows surrounding the courtyard from where the sound of soft, chanting voices floated down. A feeling of peace and tranquillity enveloped me.

As we neared the inner door, it was flung open and a small nun in a brown habit came towards us with her arms outstretched. Her bright eyes smiled, she nodded and indicated that we follow her up a stone staircase into a huge dormitory lined with beds and cots, made up with clean linen.

'It is Heaven,' I murmured, reassured by the crucifix on the white wall.

Several novices saw our state, ran off and fetched three large, white, round, enamel bowls, filled with warm water with extra jugs at the side.

'Let the girls wash first,' said Yuli, who organised leaders to pull screens around for privacy.

The serene, smiling nuns seemed only to be able to speak Rumanian. Making sign language, they handed each of us white shifts and pairs of knickers.

'This *is* Heaven!' we said to each other as they handed us soap and towels.

We took off our filthy clothes and plunged our arms into the soft, warm water. We cleaned our hands and arms, faces and tops. We wanted to wash away every scrap of dirt.

'Bend over the bowl and I'll wash your hair for you,' offered Julie, after she had rinsed her short crop. 'Undo your plaits.'

I unbound my grey-looking hair and put my head down for her to lather.

She poured a jug of warm water over my head for the first soaping and was just about to start when she shrieked, 'I can't do it! I can't!'

'Why can't you?'

My voice was muffled over the basin.

'You have too many lice!'

I raised my head. As the water trickled into the bowl, hundreds of live creatures appeared, swimming and drowning in the water.

'Get them out!' I screamed.

The nuns brought extra bowls of water and helped to wash my hair again . . . and again . . . and then again. After that, a nun who spoke Polish brought a small, metal comb and gently combed through my long hair, picking out the lice and putting them back in the water.

'This will kill them off,' she said eventually, dousing my hair in a liquid called naphtha that smelt like petrol and rubbing it in.

That night, as I lay in a large cot, all the itching had stopped and I felt safe and clean for the first time in months.

By morning, I had lapsed into unconsciousness, running a high temperature and gasping painfully for breath. My body was covered with perspiration as I shivered uncontrollably. I had developed pneumonia.

*　*　*　*　*

In my moments of consciousness, I rasped and gasped for air. Faces peered worriedly down at me. Sometimes I felt one of the adults holding me up, encouraging me to drink, but I was too weak to respond.

In my delirium, I cried for Mamushia. They were taking me to the baths. Where was Tatush? He said he would see me soon. Grandfather appeared and shook his head at me then I was in the bathhouse again, being rubbed down by Chucha, who combed and plaited my long hair with red ribbon. Aunt Zofia was there, coaxing me to keep warm then Mr Bombala and Janina came with a cart and took me away . . . away.

'I don't want to leave!' I woke screaming. 'I don't want to go away!'

I was lost in a twilight world of memories and fear. Delirious and dying.

Kindly nuns fondled me, gently wiping my thin body with damp towels. They held cold flannels to my forehead trying to cool me. I felt them change the wringing-wet bed linen many times.

My body became even more emaciated. Julie, Shona and Rene helped the leaders to take it in turns to coax me with broth or gruel.

Sometimes, someone would come and sit by the cot and whisper, 'Come on, Genia. We are going to the land of milk and honey. Don't give up now. The war is over. We are going to the Promised Land.

But the illness took its time and it was more than three weeks before I noticed the sunlight and shadows dancing on the white walls of the dormitory. At last, the fever left me and I began to recover. I lay breathing quietly without any pain.

When I tried to lift my hands, I couldn't, I was too weak. I could hear talking at the other end of the dormitory, but when I tried to speak, I couldn't make a sound.

A rosy, round face peered over the cot. It was Shona, beaming down.

'Are you better yet?'

I managed a nod.

'She's better!' shouted Shona and everyone in the group came and crowded around and told me how pleased they were.

'About time,' said Katz.

I was far too weak to walk. The next day, Yuli wrapped me in a blanket and carried me down the stone stairs into the sunshine of the courtyard. He lifted me into a pushchair and some of the boys took turns pushing me around the well for a while.

The air was filled with busy insects, zooming and zigzagging over June meadows in search of food. I sat in the pushchair, watching the girls help a nun to draw drinking water from the well.

One of the boys called Shlomo, who had very fair skin and ginger hair, handed me a mug whilst the nun stood, smiling and nodding, as I sipped the cold, clear liquid.

The sheltered walls of the cobbled courtyard reflected the warmth of the sun. It was a safe, enclosed world, a good place to convalesce.

Josh came and sat by me.

'I'm glad you're better. We didn't think you would pull through,' he told me. 'The war's over at last, but I'll never forget. Would you like to see my stamps?'

Food was still limited. There were far too many mouths for the convent to feed. The leaders hovered around, making decisions as to who should go into the village. They returned with sacks of vegetables for soup, cabbages, sometimes flour for the nuns to bake into bread, eggs and sometimes cheese.

Very gradually, I began to regain my strength.

'I think I can walk to the well today,' I told Shona.

I hung on to her arm and with very wobbly legs managed to get myself to the raised wall of the well and look over the edge into its deep centre.

'I think it must be a magic well,' I said. 'The water has made me feel better.'

But I was still able to manage only a few steps.

'We're making plans to move,' Katz told us that evening. 'We must get to Alba Julia.'

He turned to me.

'Practise walking,' he said. 'We have to leave here by the end of June.'

*   *   *   *   *

Several nuns came into the courtyard to wave goodbye and make the sign of the cross as the large, wooden doors swung open. I started off walking, but the way back down the hillside soon became too much for me so Yuli lifted up my frail body and carried me.

We descended to the village post office and waited outside in the sun while Katz disappeared inside. Soon, several other men, who seemed to be leaders, came and joined us.

Not long afterwards, a rickety, old, single-decker bus rolled up driven by a soldier. Everybody climbed in. Yuli carried me to the back seat, laid me down and gently covered me with an overcoat.

The bus screeched into gear and jolted forward on its way around the winding roads that led up to the town of Alba Julia. The ride was so bumpy that, in one jolt, I was thrown to the floor. After that, Yuli sat and held my legs when the going became very rough.

'She's not that strong yet,' I overheard one of the leaders say to another, sitting in front of me.

'Thank goodness she recovered,' he replied, 'or we would have lost her income.'

I told Julia about it at the first stop.

'He's getting paid for me,' I said indignantly. 'If I died he wouldn't care. I'm only here because of the money!'

'It was only a joke,' said Julie, but I did not believe her.

It was clear that someone was paying for everything. The leaders never seemed to be short of purchasing power.

17. ALBA JULIA

July 1945

The bus rumbled through the streets of Alba Julia, drawing up in front of an imposing house with a large portico. Once inside the hallway our eyes nearly popped out of our heads.

The walls were decorated with huge, gilded mirrors, chandeliers hung from the ceiling, a mahogany desk stood in front of carved panelling and there was red carpet on the grand staircase.

'Go upstairs and pick your room,' ordered Katz.

The first floor consisted of bedrooms, all finely furnished with ornately decorated mirrors around the walls. Some bedrooms even had mirrors on the ceiling.

We stared open-mouthed at the opulence.

'We're billeted in an abandoned brothel,' announced Micky, coming up behind us.

'What's a brothel?' I whispered to Julie.

'It's where men go for girls,' she said knowingly.

'It's very beautiful.'

'They pay money to stay here. It's like a hotel.'

'Who's paying for us to stay?' I wanted to know.

'The Joint,' said Katz, who pushed past us to his own room. 'Aren't you lucky?'

There were enough rooms for everybody to have their own bedroom, but I could not settle to the idea of sleeping alone in a room with mirrors all round, so Shona said we could share.

What a place! Everyone's spirits lifted. When we gathered in the dining room for hot soup and potatoes, Paula started us singing a folk song and we clapped and laughed together.

Katz looked surprisingly pleased for a change and said he was going to arrange for us to look very smart for Palestine.

During the night, I woke with a start, frightened and wondering where on earth I was.

'We're in Rumania,' whispered Shona, 'waiting to go to the Holy Land. Now go back to sleep.'

The following morning, Paula went out to buy material. Later, we were measured up by a dressmaker and by the end of the week bundles of clothes were delivered and we excitedly tried on our new navy skirts and white blouses.

'It really fits me!' I exclaimed, doing up the waistband of my skirt.

It was strange to see the boys smartly dressed in neat, grey trousers and white shirts. I hardly recognised Josh. He was so proud of himself. His stomach seemed to disappear in the new trousers and he couldn't wait to get to Palestine.

'Everything will be wonderful,' he assured me, 'in the land of milk and honey,' and he danced a little dance that made me laugh out loud for the first time I could remember.

'Was it you who sat by my bed when I was ill?' I asked him, suddenly realising.

'Yes,' he replied. 'I wanted you to get better to share our new lives. I want to get there quickly, they're going to make me better too.'

The girls still only possessed one pair of knickers each, so to make sure they were clean and ready for the journey we washed them out every evening and hung them to dry overnight on a line attached to the window shutters. Every night after that we went to sleep hoping the next day would be the one we could leave for Palestine.

The long summer dragged on until one morning a photographer appeared and we each had to sit on a chair in the dining room for our picture to be taken.

'It's for your travel pass,' said Katz.

But the excitement was short-lived. News came through from Joint headquarters that ships with immigrants to Palestine had been turned back by the British authorities and escorted to Cyprus where refugees were detained in camps.

It was frightening, unreal. After all our efforts to be free, we were going to be put into a refugee camp. The group sat around discussing it, angry and forlorn.

'We'll get you there somehow,' said one of the leaders. 'Even if it has to be illegal.'

'What's legal or not legal?' Micky asked.

'Haven't we been through enough?' sighed Josh.

'Be patient,' said Katz.

*   *   *   *   *

September 1945

In the middle of September, Katz bounced into the dining room, waving a piece of paper in the air.

'I've got some news!'

We stopped eating and listened in silence as he said, 'You children have got permission to leave . . . as Jews . . . for Haifa . . . for Palestine.'

For a moment nobody spoke then large, rolling tears coursed down Julie's pale cheeks. Shona and Rene started to cry as well. Suddenly, everyone was flinging their arms around everyone else, laughing and crying at the same time.

I looked over at Josh, whose face was ecstatic, but I could only think miserably, 'I won't see Aunt Zofia or Mira ever again.'

Tears rolled down my face as well, but no one understood why.

Despite permission from the British Mandate that we children could enter Palestine, we still had to wait several weeks more in Rumania. The adult refugees who had gathered in the 'red-light' house in Alba Julia became very disgruntled with us.

'It's all right for you kids, but we still have to hang around here for Heaven knows how long,' they grumbled . . . until one day, horrific news came through.

A refugee ship, attempting to get into Palestine, had struck a mine off the coast of Turkey. It had sunk with only a handful of survivors.

'Even if we get permission, we may never reach the Holy Land,' they said despairingly.

Fear spread like fire through the group.

'What if it happens to us?' said Micky, whose tall body was beginning to fill out.

'It's worth the risk,' insisted Shlomo, running his hands through his ginger hair.

'We've died a thousand deaths already, what's one more? Who else would want us anyway?' said Josh.

'There's no going back now,' we agreed.

*　*　*　*　*

October 1945

'All okay, kids,' announced Katz after breakfast. 'You're on your way.'

We stared at one another, hardly daring to believe it was the beginning of another adventure.

'Get your bundles together, you leave in half an hour. Time for me to say goodbye. Yuli and two helpers will accompany you on board the ship. New leaders will take you over.'

We stood, waiting in the hallway, bonded together by our experiences, not wanting to leave and yet not wanting to stay.

An old army coach drew up outside the house. Katz stood beside the coach steps. He had been strict and bossy, but he had steered us to a safe harbour. Now, to our amazement, as he helped each of us up on to the coach, he hugged us.

'Safe journey and see you one day in Palestine,' he grinned.

'Shalom,' he whispered in my ear.

I wondered what it meant.

'You're coming, aren't you?' I asked Paula, standing beside Katz at the door of the coach.

'Not yet. You children are only the first batch. There are others, I have to go back.'

I hugged her despondently. She was the last link with Jagellonska 32, Apartment 32.

'Next stop Soliva, then Edirne, then Constanza,' yelled Yuli as he herded us on to tatty, old, ripped seats stuck together with bits of tape.

In our new clothes, brown, lace-up shoes and short, white socks, clutching bundles of spare shirts and blouses, we left the brothel looking like a school party on an outing, but truly we were a subdued and nervous group, uncertain of what lay ahead and wondering if we would ever see the Holy Land at all.

The coach rolled and bumped along the road.

We stopped at Soliva overnight in a large farmhouse, sharing beds and breakfasting on huge omelettes, bread and butter. Then down towards the coast.

At Edirne, the coach parked near a church by the market where we were allowed to walk around to stretch our legs. It was market day and the town bustled with people marketing farm animals: goats, hens and live fish swimming in wooden barrels.

There were live geese, with their legs tied together, squawking loudly. Stalls lined the square laden with shabby, second-hand goods or farm produce like goat's cheese, black bread and vegetables. None of us had money to buy anything but the smells and sounds excited and enthused our spirits. We felt part of humanity again.

Yuli and another leader waited for us to gather back by the coach before they set off around the stalls to buy food. The sun shone warmly on our faces as we sat patiently by the churchyard waiting for them.

It seemed ages before we spotted the two leaders coming towards us, but something was wrong. Yuli's legs did not seem to be moving properly. His companions were half-carrying, half-dragging him along. Micky and the other leader ran towards them to help. As they brought him back, his arms hung around their necks and his head was bent forward in a swoon.

I screamed with the others when we realised he was fainting with pain. His face had been punched and bruised, his eyes were swollen, a cut had split his lips and his shirt was covered in dirt and blood.

'For Heaven's sake, what's happened?' yelled the driver of the coach, taking Yuli's legs and helping to lift him into the back of the vehicle.

His friend looked shaken and pale.

'Same old story,' he said ruefully. 'Yuli was buying bread, I was at another stall for fruit. Same old words *'Juden! Juden!'* I was just able to get to him before they beat him unconscious, those thugs!'

'Why? Why?' I wailed, but there was never an answer to it.

We girls stood, shaking and trembling with terror.

'He can't travel,' called the driver from the back. 'His ribs are broken. We'll have to get him patched up.'

'I'll try the church,' said Micky, disappearing into the vestibule.

He reappeared with a priest who climbed into the coach and was horrified at Yuli's injuries.

He spoke broken German, which we understood.

'All of you, come inside the church for safety,' he said and offered to call a doctor.

The group spent that evening sitting in the pews. Yuli groaned as the priest and a leader laid him gently on a blanket on the floor of the transept. His arms were outstretched and his chest bared for the doctor to examine him.

I gazed at the crucifix above the altar.

'He looks like Jesus,' I thought.

'I don't want him to die,' I sobbed. 'Our Father, who art in Heaven, please make Yuli better.'

Two nuns were summoned to look after us whilst the doctor and leaders attended to Yuli.

The kindly nuns took the group to their small convent nearby where they fed us and arranged for us to spend the night on the floor of the dining hall, lying on blankets and coats.

The priest called in early next morning to report.

'Where's Yuli? How's Yuli?' we all wanted to know.

'He's very obstinate! God knows,' smiled the priest, folding his hands in prayer. 'He's in a lot of pain, but he insists you leave for Constanza today.'

Once again, I climbed into the coach by the convent gate, forlorn and empty at leaving Yuli. I had become attached to him. Other leaders came and went, but he was protective and strong – and there.

As I made my way to the back seat I suddenly saw Yuli lying on it, all bandaged up.

I ran along the gangway.

'You're coming with us!' I cried delightedly.

'You didn't think you could leave me behind, did you?'

He winced with pain as he spoke.

I heaved a deep sigh of relief and grinned at him.

'Hang on to my legs in case I fall off,' he reminded me with a wink.

* * * * *

At long last, someone shouted, 'Look, there's the sea!'

The Black Sea came into view as the bus turned in towards the port of Constanza.

I stared out of the window. I had never seen the sea before. It spread to the horizon, a blue strip, shimmering in the evening sunlight. It lay tranquil and calm, smooth as ice for ships to slide along.

We were let off near the docks and had to walk a fair way beside railways lines leading to the quayside. Two leaders made a chair with their arms for Yuli and carried him with his arms around their necks.

Grey fishing vessels bobbed out on the water. Seagulls swooped and dived, their harsh cries mingling with ships' sirens. Long barges were moored by the wharves, their cargoes spilling onto the docks. Everything was steeped with the salty smell of the sea.

We gradually drew nearer to the huge, black hull of passenger ship rising above us. With its pale blue, striped funnel and metal stairways, the ship lay waiting for us to board.

It was the SS Transylvania.

18. SS TRANSYLVANIA

White-coated Rumanian sailors stood smartly on deck as passengers embarked. We watched as Yuli, supported by his friends, was helped up the gangway. Then clutching our official papers we filed up behind.

A steward took the boys off to their cabins.

'Follow me, girls,' said another, who led the four of us downstairs to the lower decks.

We found ourselves in a tiny cabin with one, small porthole and four hammocks hanging from one side to the other.

'Little ones on top!' he instructed. 'Come back on deck in half an hour for food.'

Rene and I climbed up the rope ladders and tried the hammocks, which swung precariously as we fell into them. The sides hugged our bodies snugly and safely. Julie and Shona swung widely in the lower hammocks. After this fun, we all tipped ourselves onto the floor, giggling madly.

Micky put his head round the door.

'Come on, you girls. We've got a meeting upstairs.'

We left our small bundles in the cabin and followed him on deck where the rest of the group was sitting on benches eating bread and cheese and passing round a khaki water bottle to drink from.

A much older man, holding a clipboard, stood up and introduced himself.

'I'm Meyer, your new leader,' he said. 'I shall need your names and details, but not now. We've plenty of time, the journey will take several days. In the meantime, I'm here to take care of you. If there's anything you want, just ask.'

He surveyed his charges with a wry smile.

'You're allowed to look around the ship if you want. Food will be served to you once a day in the dining hall. The rest of the time, we'll meet out here for snacks. Any questions?'

'What's Palestine like? What's going to happen to us when we get there?' asked Josh eagerly with most of the others.

Meyer smiled and opened his arms to the darkening sky.

'The sky is always blue. The sun is very warm. The food is extremely good . . . and there's plenty of it. You will go to school there and you will be looked after and what is more important, no one will frighten you ever again.

We hushed up in reverent silence.

*　*　*　*　*

It was almost nightfall before preparations were made to sail. Back in the cabin, the events of the past months and the noise of the ship's engines drumming in the hold soon overcame me. It was warm enough in the hammocks to lie without blankets. For the first time in a long while, I understood I was safe at last from the horrors of war.

'We're going to the land of milk and honey,' I said thankfully. 'Goodnight.'

'Sweet dreams, goodnight!' chorused the others and we were all sound asleep before the ship started moving.

The next morning, turbulent waves buffeted the hull, sending the ship rocking from side to side.

I awoke in a violently swinging hammock, feeling extremely sick and just managed to tumble out to make my way to the top deck in time to lean over the side, along with other passengers.

'I don't want anything to eat,' I moaned to Meyer, with eyes half closed.

'Go back to bed,' he advised, looking at my green face. 'When we get out of the Black Sea all will be calm. See you later.'

One of the young leaders popped his head round the door during the morning and offered me a sip of water.

By midday, I began to feel better. The sea was calmer and I was getting used to the movement of the ship. I drifted off to sleep. When I woke, none of the others were in the cabin. I tumbled out and made my way up top.

'I'm hungry!' I announced to the world.

'Perhaps we could all eat something now,' said Meyer.

We sat on deck at the stern of the ship, where sailors brought us rolls and cheese and halves of oranges to suck. I had forgotten the wonderful, tangy taste of sweet orange juice as it trickled down my chin.

Each person was given a bottle of water for themselves.

'Keep that with you during the day. It gets hotter and you will need it,' warned Meyer. 'When it's finished you can take another one from the main kitchen.'

That evening, the group gathered together around a long table in the dining room. Stewards in white coats served hot food, which we politely ate with knives and forks. Some of us were unable to stop giggling.

After dinner, Meyer produced his clipboard files. There was one for each child. He asked everyone to fill in the first page with their name and any addresses that they could remember. Also the names of their parents and grandparents.

'I'm trying to find as much information about you as I can so we can trace your relatives,' he said. 'Tomorrow I will talk to each of you separately to see if you can tell me anymore.'

A morning heat haze lay over the calm, azure sea as Meyer walked the decks with each of the group in turn, talking, questioning:

'What was the name of your father? What was the name of your mother? Where did you live? Were you able to go to school? Were the Germans horrible to you?'

When he came to me with his clipboard to ask my name I replied at once, 'Genia Skalska . . . er . . . no . . . Rapaport.'

'Is that your real name?'

'Of course it is!' I said indignantly. 'I wrote it before.'

'Why do you call yourself 'Genia'? That's not a Jewish name.'

'It is my name!'

I felt I was under attack.

He spoke quietly, but insistently, trying to pacify me.

'Listen, lots of children had lots of names. How do I know this is your real name?'

'What name would Auntie know me by then?'

I became very agitated.

'What Auntie?'

'Aunt Zofia!'

'Who's Aunt Zofia?'

'I love her,' I sobbed. 'She saved my life. I want to go back!'

He was very concerned that I was so upset.

'Look, I'm choosing a very nice place for you to live. I just want details of you.'

'Why? Why are you asking me all these questions?' I screamed rudely. 'What are you trying to make me say? Am I going to prison camp?'

'Of course not,' he replied calmly. 'You're going to a lovely farm settlement called Petach Tikvah, near Tel Aviv. Calm down now. Tell me all about Aunt Zofia.'

He listened patiently, sometimes taking notes, occasionally asking a question as I retold as much as I could, from the Ghetto in Radom to the end of the war, including everything about the Grudzinski family that I remembered.

'So – you are really Goldie Rapaport. Your father is Simon and your mother is Rachel. Your grandfather, David, owned the timber yard in Radom. Your birthday is on 23rd January and you are now eleven years old. Is that right?

'Yes,' I whispered, 'but please write me down as Genia so my Auntie will know where to find me.'

After the retelling I felt empty and bereft . . . like all the others who had lost the love and safety of their families.

Always I yearned for Aunt Zofia's comforting arms.

By midday, the sun was so hot that the back of Shlomo's neck was redder than his hair. My fair skin was burning. We were told to douse ourselves with water and go inside for food. There was more than enough to eat on the ship as it sailed away from the horrors of Eastern Europe.

Meyer gleaned as much as he could from the twelve of us and was now well aware of our sufferings. He kept repeating how lucky we were to be on the ship.

'On the very first legal ship from Rumania to be allowed to dock in Haifa. Some grown-ups do not possess legal papers like you.'

He encouraged us to be cheerful.

'Watch the horizon tonight,' he said. 'Soon you will see the lights of Haifa twinkling in the dark. It's very beautiful.'

'When we see them, will we be there?' I sighed.

Everyone became very excited about spotting the lights in the distance. We kept awake all night, to go up onto the deck in turns, so as not to miss the first sight of Haifa, but by the time the ship drew near enough, it was daybreak and the twinkling myriads of lights had vanished in the grey mist of dawn.

It was not until the sun came up over the sea, its rays lighting the sky beyond the horizon, that the SS Transylvania steered majestically into harbour, sounding her siren.

Skilfully, she was manoeuvred into place by two pilot tugs, during which time our eagerness gradually waned because it took so long for her dock.

We were not allowed to disembark before officials boarded to take details. A smiling, dark-skinned man, with a huge, wooden platter hanging from straps round his shoulder, brought refreshments from shore. Rolls of jam or cheese were handed round and I helped myself to bread dipped in olive oil and garlic which looked good, but it tasted so peculiar that I spat it out.

By nine-thirty, a very bronzed, elderly gentleman boarded the ship with several other people. He was clean-shaven and although he only wore khaki shorts with a light blue shirt, he seemed to be an important official.

He sat on one of the benches with us around him in a semi-circle.

'We are from Youth Aliyah and Sochnut,' he said. 'We need to know everything about you all so that we can send you to the right places for your education.'

Once again, people took each child aside and questioned them. Every one of us already had documented pages held together with green tags.

He beckoned me to sit by him. In his hands were my file and the entry permit with my photo.

'Is this really you?' he asked me in Polish.

'What do you mean, sir?'

'No, I'm not sir . . . my name is Asher. Tell me about yourself. What's your name?'

The interrogation was starting all over again.

'I've already told my name.' I pointed rudely to the paper. 'It's written there.'

'Don't be upset,' he went on kindly. 'We're here to help you. To get you resettled as quickly as possible. Maybe find some of your family for you.'

He paused as he looked at the notes.

'Why do you keep asking me the same things over and over again? It's there!'

I was getting upset again.

'I just want to be sure,' Asher replied.

'Who am I going with? Can I stay with Julie, Rene and Shona?'

'We'll keep you together, yes, until you're a bit older. First you have to go to school.'

'I can read and write,' I offered.

'Oh yes . . . in Polish,' grinned Asher, 'but you will have to learn Hebrew.'

That stunned me. Not only was I going to a strange country where I didn't know a soul, no one was going to understand a word I said. I had never imagined that.

The heat was unbearable on deck. I was being burnt by the minute. Suddenly, a little band of recorders and an accordion struck up on the quayside. Looking over the side, we could see people waving blue and white flags.

We collected our little bundles and hid jam rolls inside, just in case.

'Be proud,' called Meyer. 'You are the first legal immigrants. Off you go. Good luck!'

We trundled down the gangplank behind Asher, one after the other. As we neared the band, we saw it was composed of children, playing *'Havainuh shalom alechem'* (we bring peace upon you) over and over again.

The quayside was packed with excited people waiting to welcome us as we disembarked. The ship's siren sounded again, people hugged and kissed us and said things we couldn't understand.

Several grown-ups were crying. The group stood together, looking bewildered, finding it impossible to respond.

After some kind of official welcome, Asher led us to a waiting grey Egged bus, ready to drive us away to the unknown. I was sad that I had not seen Yuli that morning to say 'goodbye'.

There was no surge of excitement in me. I sat next to Shona on the bus and looked across at Julie and Rene. They did not seem very happy either. The only two people smiling away were the bus driver and Josh.

The bus rattled up the hill from the port and through the outskirts of Haifa, past apartments and town houses to where orange groves bordered the dusty road. The scorched land was dotted with lush, green patches.

We sped along the coast road and an hour later arrived at the settlement of Meshek Ha-po-alot, just north of Tel Aviv.

19. THE MESHEK

The afternoon heat hit my face when the door of the bus opened. The driver told the boys to stay where they were, since they were to be taken to another working farm.

'But we thought we would be together,' we cried.

'You will, after your weeks of training, but this is a women's farm . . . so, boys, you can't stay here!'

Oddly enough, having to split up seemed to upset us more than anything.

'You'll meet soon, don't worry,' said the driver.

The heat wrapped around us as we four girls stepped down from the bus. Several ladies, standing in the shade, came forward to greet us.

'Welcome to the Meshek!'

The compound seemed very quiet and sleepy.

'Come with me,' a petite lady with a soft-spoken voice said in Polish. 'I am taking charge of you.'

She led us inside a modern, two-storey building. In the hallway, white walls and tiled floors made it pleasantly cool.

'My name is Tova . . . you know, that means 'good'.'

She spoke so softly we had to strain to hear her.

'May I have your papers? So . . . you are Rene, Shona, Julie and Genia.'

She pointed to each of us in turn.

'Is that right?'

We nodded.

'I'm here to help you and look after you. If you do what I say your lives will be comfortable and happy, but I have to be honest, you are going to have to work hard.'

We glanced at each other apprehensively. The last thing we wanted, in our mental and physical state of exhaustion, was work.

'You must be hot and sticky . . . so first you can wash yourselves.'

Tova took the grubby four of us to shower rooms where toilets and cubicles were spotlessly clean.

'Undress,' she ordered.

We each had a shower cubicle and Tova stood between us saying, 'Now wash your hair, now wash your bottom. Here's a special brush to wash your back.'

I had never had a shower before and I stood, blissfully letting cool water stream down over my head and body. It was a glorious sensation.

When she was quite satisfied we were clean, Tova handed out soft, white towels.

She studied my emaciated little body as she laid out neat piles of clean clothing.

'They won't fit you just yet, but you'll soon grow into a big girl, Gina.'

'Gina? My name's Genia,' I protested.

Tova laughed.

'Gina is Hebrew for Genia,' she said.

'But I wanted Genia. I told them on the ship!'

'Well,' said Tova, 'I shall still call you Genia when I talk to you in Polish, but you will have to learn Hebrew from now so . . . it's Gina. Okay?'

After that, we got dressed in new, white vests and knickers, white, sleeveless tops and blue skirts. Tova showed us how to button the two flaps on the skirt into an overtop which could be let down if we were too hot.

'How smart you are,' she approved. 'Now we'll put your old clothes and bundles into the launderette.'

Before I could protest that everything in my bundle was clean anyway – especially the roll I had been hiding for later, the bundles were scooped up and sent down a chute.

'But . . .' I started.

'No buts,' said Tova, sounding exactly like Katz. 'Everything must be sterilised or the chickens might fall ill, the cows might fall ill, even we might fall ill.'

'But I had photos in my pocket,' I wailed.

'No, you didn't,' said Tova. 'I already took them out. Here you are.'

I clutched my photos and saw even our brown lace-ups popped down the chute.

'These are much cooler for you to wear,' said Tova, offering us each a pair of wooden clogs.

What a racket they made on the stone floor as we tried to walk!

'Not such a noise!' Tova hushed my clatter. 'Look, glide, slide along like this.'

The clogs were miles too big for my small feet but, strangely, they were very comfortable in the heat.

'In no time you'll grow into them,' smiled Tova. 'Now I'll show you around.'

Upstairs was a dormitory where four girls could sleep together in one room.

After that, with damp hair still clinging to our necks, she took us out into the scorching sun. We followed her around in silence.

I was intrigued by the settlement. Everything had its place. Nothing was higgledy piggledy like Dziadek's farm.

'Here are the chickens, here are the cows. Over there is the barn . . . and here is where we eat . . . the dining room.'

We peered inside at rows of clean, long tables and benches.

'It's almost suppertime,' said Tova.

'I'm starving,' I thought, still mad because my roll and jam had been thrown into the wash.

'Are you ready to eat?' asked Tova.

Early diners turned to look at the new arrivals. Such pale, skinny children.

'Why are they staring as if something's wrong with me?' I thought resentfully. 'I'm not from the moon!'

But I may well have been. I simply could not believe the abundance of food laid out in the centre of each table. At the very minute we sat down, we girls grabbed at the bread and butter, cheese and fruit and tucked in without another word.

But that was not all. People came up and served huge plates of hot potatoes and lamb stew . . . more food than I had ever eaten in my life. It was fantastic. We couldn't stop eating and no one stopped us.

Of course, it was bad to put so much food into shrunken stomachs. Within hours, we were vomiting and suffering from diarrhoea, hopelessly in pain from eating too much.

All during the next day, Tova tended us as we lay in bed feeling sorry for ourselves.

'You don't have to eat,' she said, 'but it's good for you to keep drinking.'

Every half an hour or so, she supplied sweet, lukewarm tea, encouraging us to drink up to prevent dehydration. My bottom became so sore I could not sit on it.

'It's awful here,' I moaned, longing for Aunt Zofia's comfort. 'I want to go home.'

'This is home,' whispered Shona.

It took a couple of days to recover. We lay under trees in the shade during the mornings. We were allowed to go into the dining room whenever we liked, but we still found it difficult not to eat everything we saw. Gradually, we learned just how much our stomachs could cope with and began to feel better.

On Friday evening, we met up with the boys again for Sabbath. That night, in the dining hall, all the group watched as candles were lit on each table and the Sabbath prayer was said. Mamushia and Grandfather seemed very near.

After a satisfying meal, we exchanged news. The boys, too, had been suffering with their stomachs. Especially Josh, who looked very ill.

'I've had a dreadful time,' he told me. 'I think they are going to take me to hospital next week to operate.'

'That will be good.'

I was pleased for him.

'At last you will be better.'

'Will you keep something safe for me?'

'Of course.'

'I don't want anyone else to have them,' he said, handing me his book of stamps.

*　*　*　*　*

We were left to recuperate for the first ten days, laying in bed through the early morning, listening to the noises of the farm; joining the workers at mealtimes and wandering around the compound in the heat of the afternoon, or lounging around in the common room, with the radio on, when everyone else was taking a siesta.

'Now that you're better,' said Tova eventually, 'you can help in the fields tomorrow.'

It was still dark when we were woken. Tova handed us khaki trousers and shirts.

'It's only 4am!' we complained. 'Why do we have to get up so early?'

'You'll see,' said Tova. 'Follow me. You'll need hats.'

She plonked a white cloth hat on my head.

Other workers spilled out into the campus moving off in different directions.

By the time we had walked for fifteen minutes to the cornfield, it was just becoming light and the first bird was tuning up for the dawn chorus.

We were each given a hoe and shown how to weed spaces between the corn, twelve inches apart. Tova worked alongside us.

The sun's rays intensified. As we moved slowly along the rows, our shadows changed the colour of the earth. It was becoming hotter than I had ever experienced.

'Even if you're hot, don't remove your shirts,' advised Tova. 'You'll get sunburnt. It can kill you.'

Just before eight, when we were sweating with the heat, a distant bell sounded from the dining hall.

'Breakfast!' announced Tova.

The tables truly were laden with milk and honey.

'Won't Josh be pleased – he was right!' I thought, wondering how he was.

On the side tables were fruits, semolina, hot rolls or toast, olives, curd cheese, goat cheese, salads, sweet herrings, cucumbers, eggs and Smetana (like yoghurt) that you could pour onto anything. It was all delicious.

'Help yourselves,' said Tova.

This time we were more careful. I started by choosing the scrambled egg, but didn't like the texture, so I swapped it for a boiled egg. Then I copied Tova and tried tomatoes with Smetana then I ate bread and honey, drank a glass of milk . . . then I stopped.

'You'll put on weight in no time,' laughed Tova. 'Sit quietly and let it go down for quarter of an hour . . . we'll be going to the orange groves next.'

A tractor pulled us way down the hillside, sitting in a cart with other workers. The groves were irrigated by ditches on one side and the trees were laden with ripe oranges.

'You each have a quota,' shouted the woman in charge. 'You need to pick twenty bags full, then you can rest.'

Sacking bags were distributed.

She held back the newcomers and showed us how to use the bags for collecting fruit.

'These hold about forty oranges,' she said. 'When they are filled you open them at the bottom, see?'

She demonstrated.

'Two bags fill one orange box.'

She placed a bag over my thin shoulders.

It was hard work. Forty oranges were not difficult to pick, but extremely heavy to carry. I heaved the first bagful over to the box but some fell on the ground as I tipped them out.

'Watch out!' the supervisor shouted angrily. 'They go for export. They must be perfect!'

Once or twice I accidently dropped an orange on the damp soil and got told off again .

'I don't like doing this one bit,' I thought.

That night I took paper and pencil from the library room and wrote a long letter to Aunt Zofia and Mira.

'It's awful here,' I wrote. *'As soon as I save up enough money, I'm coming straight back to you!'*

* * * * *

The daily routine continued. By the time I finished my quota the sun was burning in the midday sky, beating and scorching any unprotected place. Even though the groves were shaded and cooler than the fields, the humidity was very high and everyone was soaked in sweat like a Turkish bath.

When the truck returned to take us for lunch there was always a rush for the showers.

'I'll be late if I have to wait my turn,' I worried. 'I'll miss all the food!'

But that never happened. No matter what time we arrived in the dining hall, food was always there. Gradually, the panic that comes from experiencing starvation began to wear off.

At first, we were unable to sleep during siesta, but after working alongside the others we gladly joined in with the rest of the compound, drifting into dreamland as we lay, supine and naked, on our beds. That was the end of the working day.

Late in the afternoon, Tova introduced us to her friend, Allon. He was a teacher and came to test us for Hebrew groups. Rene, who turned out to be very intelligent, was placed in the 'good' team with Allon. Shona, Julie and I were taught by Tova.

Two hours of drilling with the alphabet and trying to make sense of the strange writing left me absolutely fed up.

'I don't want to learn Hebrew!'

I fought off any attempt to be taught Ivrit, but Tova was very patient and kind. Despite myself, I soon picked up sayings like:

'Ken' (Yes),
'Lo' (No),
'Boker Tov' (Good Morning) and
'Toda' (Thank You).

'I'll try these out on the boys tomorrow.'

Despite myself, I felt pleased with my progress.

On Friday nights, candles were lit on the main table in the dining hall and the Sabbath prayer was said over the wine and bread. Every time this happened, something stirred in my heart and made me feel I was at home.

When the boys came over again, there were only six of them.

'Where's Shlomo and Josh?' I asked.

Micky's good-looking face twisted and he looked uncomfortable.

'Shlomo's got sunstroke,' volunteered one of the others.

Micky said, 'Gina, I've something to tell you. Come near.'

The others turned away as I sat by him, wondering what was so secret.

'Well?'

'Josh is dead.'

'No! He can't be!' I screamed, jumping up in anguish.

'Sit down, listen.' Micky grabbed my arm. 'He was very ill. You know that, don't you?'

'Yes.'

I was crying uncontrollably.

'He was happy to have the operation. He knew it was his only chance . . . he died on the operating table.'

'This is an awful place! He came here to die!' I wept.

'No, that's not true,' Micky went on. 'He came here to live again and he got here, that's the important thing. Thousands, millions didn't. Come on, Gina, we've got a chance here.'

I shook my head dumbly. I couldn't see any reason in it, why he should suffer only to die.

'He can lie in the sun and be forever in our land of milk and honey,' Micky said.

'Is it our land?'
I was calming down through the tears.
'Don't you know anything about our history?'
Micky was astonished.
'No,' I said.

* * * * *

Josh's death left me feeling more lonely than ever. It seemed that whenever you got close to someone, liked them, loved them even, they disappeared or died or you had to leave them.

The girls were friends, but Josh had been special because he had trusted me and shared his secrets and his special book with me.

I had nothing to call my own. I went alone to the dormitory to sit desolately on the bed and think about the past and all the travels and adventures that had brought me to the Meshek.

After a while, I lifted the stamp book from my locker and took out the photos I had carefully placed inside. I stared at the faces of the Grudzinski family, Uncle Leon, Zoshienka, Stefan, Mira and beloved Aunt Zofia.

'Will I ever see you again?' I sobbed as if my heart would break.

* * * * *

Autumn 1945

The Hebrew lessons continued every evening. Afterwards, Allon would change with Tova and tell Bible stories or elaborate on the history of the Jews. It was all astonishing. I thought that the Jews had started with killing Jesus . . . that was what made them Jews. Wasn't it?

Little by little I began to understand this was not so. I learned about the stories of Abraham, Isaac and Jacob . . . about

Moses and the land of the Pharaohs, about the exodus from Egypt into the wilderness, about the kingdoms of Israel and Judea, about King David and the psalms that he wrote, about the Romans and their punishment of crucifixion for anybody who disobeyed them. About the dispersion of people to the four corners of the earth to become stateless, undefended, unwanted refugees. And most amazing of all, that Jesus, who hung on a cross in St Floriana's church in Warsaw, was himself a Jew. I was speechless. None of it made sense and yet everything made sense.

'Is it all right to say 'Our Father'?' I asked Allon one evening during lessons.

'It is mostly a Jewish prayer,' was the reply. 'But you can learn 'Hear O Israel' as well.'

20. TATUSH

We became acclimatised to our new life. Our skins began to darken and our bodies filled out.

Within a month, Julie, Shona and Rene had picked up Hebrew quite well. They could read short children's stories printed in block capitals and understand some of the words. They seemed eager to want to speak their new language.

On the other hand, I hardly made any effort to try. I kept thinking, 'If I don't bother to learn, they'll send me back to Poland and Aunt Zofia.'

I made a pact with myself that I would not read anything aloud in class, even if they pleaded. Even if they became angry and told me off. My one aim was to be sent back.

Tova simply said, 'All right, if you don't want to learn yet . . .' and left it at that.

*   *   *   *   *

By the end of November, the days were cooler and the nights longer. We were in our room, preparing to go down to supper, when Tova's voice came from downstairs.

She was calling me in Polish.

'Genia, Genia, someone wants to see you.'

For one moment I madly thought, 'Mira has come to take me home.'

I hung over the banisters and looked down into the hallway. A man in a British soldier's uniform, his beret tucked under his shoulder tab, stood, staring up at me.

Time fell away, the years melted like snow in the heat.

Everything, everyone was forgotten as I cried, 'Tatush! Tatush!' and raced down the stairs.

I reached the bottom, about to throw myself into his arms, when he took a step backwards. I stopped in my tracks, not knowing what to do. He seemed surprised, puzzled. He didn't seem to recognise me.

I stood there wanting to fling myself at him, but he seemed so distant.

'We have to talk.' He turned to Tova. 'May I take her out?'

'Yes, of course, but she must be back by nine.'

'I'll just take her down the road to Petach Tikvah.'

He spoke as if I were a stranger.

'Will you come with me?'

'Of course,' I replied.

Side by side, we left the Meshek and walked down the road to the centre of the little village.

Questions came: 'What's your name? What's your surname?'

I was shocked.

'Don't you know me?'

I could not believe my own father did not know who I was.

'I have to make sure you're the right person,' he said. 'Tell me, how did you get out of the Ghetto?'

'You lifted me out through a window. Don't you remember?'

This was silly. How could he not know?

'Who did you go with?'

'I went with Janina.'

'Where did you go to?'

'I went to Warsaw.'

'Go on. Tell me everything you remember.'

'Don't you remember Grandfather? His log cabin? Zygmund and . . . and . . .'

I began to break down. It wasn't how I thought it should be.

From the expression on his face, the memories were too much for him as well. I said nothing of Mamushia.

'And you helped me to get away . . . Tatush . . . didn't you?'

'Goldie?'

He took my hand.

'Oh, Daddy!'

I wanted to hug him but somehow we were both too embarrassed.

He found a bench where we could sit together.

'Now that I've found you, I am afraid it won't be for long,' he said. 'I'm travelling back to Egypt tomorrow where I serve in the British Army.'

He shook his head.

'I haven't enough money to take you with me or bring you up. I'm sorry, I shall have to leave you here.'

'It's all right,' I said. 'I'm almost grown up now.'

'I can see that,' he smiled. 'You know, I didn't recognise you!'

'We can write to each other, can't we?'

'Of course. I'll give you my address. You'll be resettled from here sometime. Let me know wherever you go and I'll try to get back to you as soon and as often as I can. I promise. Is there anything you need?' he asked. 'I've got a little money on me. Anything in particular? Any food?'

'No more food!' I laughed. 'I do need a pen though.'

'Come on, then.'

We found a little tobacconist shop that was still open. On display, on the counter, were writing materials from which my father selected a fountain pen and solemnly handed it to me.

'Tatush, it's my first real own possession,' I breathed delightedly. 'I want to use it straight away.'

'Well, perhaps you can use it in your Hebrew lessons,' he said pointedly.

He seemed to know something about my behaviour. I pulled a face.

'I'll write letters,' I said.

He walked me back to the compound.

'Well, goodbye,' he began and suddenly we were in each other's arms, hugging and kissing.

'You're not alone anymore,' he whispered.

'Daddy, thank you for finding me.'

He nodded, full of emotion, then turned and left.

The girls were waiting up for me.

'Who was that? Where have you been? Was it your father?'

All their questions came together.

'Yes, it was my father.'

After all those years, I could hardly believe it.

'Is he going to take you away?'

'No.'

'I wish I had someone . . . anyone,' said Julie.

'You are lucky,' said Shona.

'If only my father would come and get me,' cried Rene, throwing herself on the bed and sobbing uncontrollably. Then they all started to weep.

'You can share him with me,' I offered.

'It's not the same!' said Rene unhappily.

They were all so upset that I kept quiet about my new pen.

* * * * *

January 1946

Six weeks later, we said farewell to Tova and Allon.

'Shalom!' we called as we left the agricultural school to join the boys at a Kibbutz in a place called Gan-Shmeul.

It was the 23rd January, 1946. My twelfth birthday.

They held a reunion dance that evening on the Kibbutz for the newcomers. As the sun went down, people sang and danced *'Shalom Aleinu'*. Micky pulled me along with the group and we all joined in to dance the *Hora*.

It came to me suddenly then that Aunt Zofia had been right all along. I did belong here, part of the new people of Israel. Part of a vibrant throng who had come through history's most evil period.

'Shalom Aleinu,' I sang.

'We bring you peace,' I danced, clapping my hands with the others.

* * * * *

That night, in my own room, in the new quarters, I carefully unpacked my belongings, my clothes and Hebrew books. I put a letter from Tatush carefully inside my Bible and pinned the photos of the Grudzinski family to the board on the wall; I placed Josh's album in my locker and then sat on the bed to write another letter to Mira and Aunt Zofia with the good news.

I fondled the pen that Tatush had bought, feeling its shiny, smooth surface and said to myself, 'One day, I shall write my story with it.'

EPILOGUE

Grandfather and Chucha died in the Holocaust. Mamushia died in Ma Becky's shop where she and the remaining members of her family gassed themselves on 20th August 1942. That night, at 12am, the Nazis began the final liquidation of the Radom Ghetto.*

Uncle Leon did not survive the war. He was taken deep into Germany where he was lost without trace.

Stefan returned from concentration camp to Warsaw at the end of April 1945. He is married with two children and lives in Lodz, Poland. He works for the United Nations as an eminent biochemist.

Zbyszek survived the war and is happily married living in Warsaw.

Sebastian returned safely from the war and married Mira. They have a son and daughter and live in Sopot, Poland. Sebastian sadly died in 1992.

After the war, Poland became part of the Communist bloc. It was impossible for Gina to go back to visit. She faithfully kept in touch with Mira and Aunt Zofia by post, sending news and photos of her family. Aunt Zofia sadly died in 1976 before Gina could see her again.

The State of Israel was declared in May 1948.

Gina remained there with Tatush until he decided to emigrate to America. She then came to England, where she met and fell in love with a young Israeli, David Schwarzmann, a lecturer in mathematics. They married in 1960 and have four, grown-up children, Jonathan, Rachelle, Danny and Nimrod.

This story is for them and their children's children.

In April 1990, Gina flew to Warsaw with her daughter, Rachelle and her friend, Evelyn Kent. She was reunited with Mira, Sebastian, Stefan and Zbyszek. They made the journey back to Radom by car and visited all the places of Gina's past.

Very little had changed. The years fell away as the Grudzinski family once more took 'Genia' into their hearts.

This story is a tribute to their friendship and courage, without which Gina would not have survived to tell her story.

A Memorial to the Jewish Community of Radom, Poland by Irgun Yotzei (Israel 1961)

PROGRESS OF THE WAR

against which background this story is set

1939

1 September	Germany invades Poland.
3 September	Britain declared war on Germany.
8 September	German armoured divisions reach outskirts of Warsaw.
27 September	Warsaw falls to Germans. Heydrich appointed to 'liquidate' all Jewish people in Poland.
3 October	Polish economy to be minimum necessary for bare existence.

1940

March	Radom Ghetto established.
April	German invasion of Norway and Denmark.
May	German invasion of Belgium and Holland.
June	Auschwitz (near Krakow) officially opened.

1942

January	Polish Workers' Party formed in alliance with Soviet Union to fight occupying power. Germans push towards Stalingrad.
July-October	Warsaw Ghetto 'Resettlement' for inmates to Treblinka where 310,322 were gassed.
23 October	El Alamein, Rommel defeated in North Africa.

1943

2 February	Stalingrad: German Sixth Army surrenders. In Poland new food scheme deprives half a million people in Warsaw suburbs of food. 60,000 Jews walled up in the Warsaw Ghetto. Severe overcrowding and no food.
19 April	Jewish inmates decide to resist and hold out for four weeks.
16 May	End of resistance in Warsaw.
3 September	Allied troops land in Southern Italy.

1944

14 April	Zoshienka and Stefan captured.
6 June	D-Day. Allied landings in Normandy.
July	Red Army advances towards Warsaw.
1 August	Polish uprising explodes. Poles hold on to Old Town until 24 September. German advance is relentless. Warsaw is razed to the ground.
2 October	Polish uprising finally crushed by Germans. Russians fail to advance to help them. Over 200,000 civilians and 15,000 Polish resistance dead.

1945

12-15 January	Russians liberate Radom.
17 January	Warsaw liberated by Russians.
7 March	US troops cross Rhine at Remagen.
16 April	US troops reach Nuremberg.
21 April	Red Army reaches outskirts of Berlin.
25 April	Patrols of US 69th Division meet Russian 58th Guards Division at Torgau on the Elbe. Northern and Southern Germany split in two.
7 May	Germany surrenders unconditionally.
8-9 May	Guns cease firing in Europe.

Other Biographies by E.J. Kent

EVA'S STORY
(A survivor's tale by the Step-sister of Anne Frank)
ISBN 09523716 93

MINA'S MOUNTAIN
Set in Wartime Austria
ISBN 09523716 69

MY FATHER'S DREAM
Palestine under the British Mandate
ISBN 09523716 85